**DIANA**
GËLLÇI

# GJAKMARRJA

# ALBANIAN
## HIGHLANDER'S
## SOCIAL OBLIGATION

# SECOND EDITION

ISBN-13: 978-1497578463

ISBN-10: 1497578469

# CONTENTS

## I.
Introduction .......................................................... 5

## II.
The traditional social structure ............................................. 12
    The member as the group representative ...................... 15
    The shtëpia - group ........................................................ 17
    The dual role of group ................................................... 19
    Brotherhood ................................................................. 22
    Vllaznia- separated brothers............................................ 22
    Vllami- brother by choice............................................... 23
    Kumbara- the spiritual brotherhood ............................ 24
    The dual role of female .................................................. 25

## III.
The albanian "old spirit".................................................. 29
    Nderi (honor)................................................................ 30
    Free to be honored........................................................ 30
    The Obligation of Being Honored................................ 33
    Mikpritja ( Hospitality).................................................. 37
    Besa- mutual social agreement...................................... 38
    Beja (oath).................................................................... 41
    The principles .............................................................. 43

## IV.

Between killing and reconciliation .......................................... 45
    Honor or fatality? ................................................................. 45
    Të biesh në gjak- To fall in blood .................................... 47
    April-love, April-death *... ................................................. 50
    Reconciliation ..................................................................... 53

## V.

The anthropology of gjakmarrja (conclusions).................. 57

## VI.

Epilogue.............................................................................. 65

## VII.

Appendix.............................................................................. 68
    Key Albanian words: ......................................................... 68

## VIII.

Bibliography ...................................................................... 70
    Gjakmarrja, Albanian Highlander's
    "Blood Feud" as Social Obligation .............................. 73
    The collection of the kanún in the 15th century............ 74
    Oral tradition and written edition .................................. 74
    Catholic influence.............................................................. 75
    Balance accounts. Mediation ........................................... 75
    Diana Gellçi's sources...................................................... 76
    The Kadaré novel ............................................................. 76
    Family................................................................................. 77
    Kanún today?..................................................................... 78
    Customary law and government ..................................... 78
    The Danish history ........................................................... 79
    The Albanian history ....................................................... 80
    Pillars of the Kanun.......................................................... 82
    LEKË DUKAGJINI (1410-1481)...................................... 84

# I

## INTRODUCTION

In the late 1990's, during the painful transition from a highly centralized economy to a free market, among other economical, political, and social problems, *gjakmarrja (gjak-* blood, *marrja*-taking) is presented by Albanian media as a returning issue for Albanian highlanders. Among hundreds of families, the reconsideration and redistribution of private properties have brought new feuds and murders resulting in male members having to stay inside of their houses totally forbidden any social activity in order to avoid death. They do not even dare working. Regarding blood feuds, the domestic media usually blames the weakness of state, the power of which more than once is reported partially replaced by the older practice of self-governance in reproducing a very old custom called *gjakmarrja* (blood taking). Some scholars blame *shpirtin e egër shqiptar* (the Albanian "fierce" spirit). Some others blame the "archaic" Albanian culture that seems not "fitting" to the new culture of capitalism. As an anthropologist, I contend there is a big gap between what was traditionally practiced and what is currently known as *gjakmarrja.*

*Gjakmarrja,* variously translated as "blood feud" or "vendetta", is an old social phenomenon traditionally well known among Albanian highlanders. Saying *blood feud or vendetta,* an American reader might think in terms of the famous stories of blood feud of Appalachia and Texas. Indeed they are similar in terms of people belonging to different clans that in given circumstances hold the free license to kill each other. However, it should be added that the blood feud stories of Texas and *gjakmarrja* would be similar only on their apparent idea of blood taken. Exactly at this point, they also ultimately diverge from each other. By the end of this essay, I hope, the reader will understand that the essential difference is not just a matter of translation. They are completely different in any other meanings. The biggest difference stands on their different cultural soil. Thus, I will continue to use the Albanian term as the best translation is inadequate.

Other forms of *gjakmarrja* have been known since Antiquity. The most famous dramas from ancient Greek and Roman times and also Shakespeare's works hinge on conflicts of the social sentiment of vendetta. However, Albanian *gjakmarrja* was a form of social obligation in a society without state's power in the picture. On the other hand, although *gjakmarrja* is not fully documented in scholars' works, it is at least as old. From my understanding, what is already documented might be considered as the sunset of *gjakmarrja,* which earlier came as a need of surviving in a system based on equality, reciprocity, solidarity, and self-governance where the individual would have survived only as belonging to a specific group. Built on a very slow-changing structure, *gjakmarrja* would have passed through all stations of maturity as successfully used, exhausted, corrupted, and maybe misused. At this point, it might have been around the 15th Century (time during which Lekë Dukagjini is recorded alive) where *gjakmarrja* was enforced through the customary law or the Code of *Lekë Dukagjini*.

The Code was first collected and published as a set of unwritten laws in 1933 by Father Shtjefen Gjeçovi. It remains a very strong and important reference affecting the Albanian highlanders' life, at least since the 15-th Century. Until recently highlanders used to refer to him as, "The Kanun said...". Even though Lekë is thought to be "an older contemporary of Scanderbeg, the national hero of modern Albania" (Hasluck, M. p,13), there is very little known about Lekë Dukagjini himself. However, instead of originating the laws, it is most likely that Lekë Dukagjini was in charge of resetting the customary laws. It is critical to understand that the Kanun has dominated and ruled the Albanian highlanders but not by state force. Rather the Kanun seems to have managed to play the reference mostly becoming part of the Albanian culture.

This set of unwritten laws remained as the strongest reference in the Albanian highlanders until recently when the traditional socio-cultural matrix has gradually changed developing into a new structure replacing the self-governance with the power of state. Then, it seems the web-obligation built on this structure lost its redefined functions until over time developing into a new structure and superstructure. What is found after that, instead of the sacred powerful institutions known as *nderi* (honor), *besa* (code of honor), *mikpritja* (hospitality), *beja* (oath), and *gjakmarrja* ( blood taking) is related to their cultural fossils. It seems that even after losing their functions, society continued to practice them just for the sake of maintaining tradition or culture.

*Gjakmarrja* appears as a total social fact (Durkheim: 1971) closely tied to the socio-cultural matrix of traditional Albanian life. Indeed, this social structure with its functions, and the dynamic of intra and inter group relations woven into the web-obligation are the soil of *gjakmarrja*. Since they collapsed a long time ago, it seems that *gjakmarrja* was reduced from a social obligation to a cultural tradition. As an integral social transaction, *gjakmarrja* traditionally played an institutional role in society, born as social obligation and matured until it lost its entire function. Finally, what is currently called *gjakmarrja* has nothing but its name in common with the highlanders' tradition usage. I want to prove that there is no connection at all between the traditional *gjakmarrja* and the practice of this crime called as *gjakmarrja* today. This essay is only a part of my study; the part that anthropologically explains how, why, where, and when *gjakmarrja* appeared as a social obligation among the Albanian highlanders. There are different reasons why Anthropology best explains the practice. First of all, *gjakmarrja* was culturally designed. Secondly, gjakmarrja was culturally learned. Finally, as I shall explain, gjakmarrja was a community's social obligation culturally enforced to its individuals.

To refer to *gjakmarrja* in the Albanian tradition, first and foremost means a full set of beliefs, rules, and rituals. Among them, I would stress the highlander's belief that *gjakmarrja* was the social obligation of killing a person for the sake of community honor; the "one by one" rule of killing between groups; and fully prohibition of the victim's stilling and violating. *Gjakmarrja*, also, cannot be well understood outside of its own social structure uniqueness and Albanian traditional context in general. Thus, in the examination of *gjakmarrja*, I will first provide a general overview of this context following a detailed analysis of the associated affiliations and obligations.

This context was described by Broughton, who as a traveler in the Balkans, noticed:

*"Specimens of almost every sort of government are to be found in Albania. Some district and towns are commanded by one man...Others obey their elders; others are under no subjection, but each man commands his own family. The power, in some places is in abeyance; and although there is no apparent anarchy, there are no rulers..."( 1971: 141).*

The traveler said, "...although there is no apparent anarchy, there are no rulers...". This sentence made me first think about the social structure (without political rulers) in Albanian traditional society. This also contrasts with the situation of Albania today where even there are rulers, Albanian society seems far from having political order. In terms of the Durkheim's theory of social cohesion, I would ask, how did the Albanian society traditionally manage to maintain the social cohesion that today seems very problematic? What was the traditional structure and how it was managed to keep social cohesion with "no rulers"? What was the function of *gjakmarrja* in the traditional Albanian structure and what role did it play in maintaining social cohesion?

To answer these questions, I will describe and analyze *gjakmarrja* in its social cultural environment among Albanian highlanders. It is in the Albanian highland, isolated by its rugged terrain, that old Albanian traditions were well preserved until recently. *Gjakmarrja* claims its own special place and function in this traditional matrix and there is no doubt it had its special role in keeping social cohesion among the Albanian highlanders. Also, Milan Sufflay a Balkans' scholar with a strong interest on the Balkan's topics, opens his book *The Serbs and The Albanians*, presuming that the social artifacts found for the Albanian highlanders are very important to the people's study in general* (p, 9). I should add that although I am Albanian, I have always been against such custom. But in studying up my own people's traditions, I finally comprehended deeper the meaning of gjakmarrja. I also realized that many things, previously very familiar to me had an importance I never fully understood. Certainly, there is much to be studied in Albanian culture from an anthropological perspective.

In order to include and elaborate all these essential features of gjakmarrja that I find to be important, this essay is organized in six parts. Chapter I is the "Introduction" of this essay. Chapter II "The Traditional Social Structure" is a description and analysis of the traditional social network among the Albanian highlanders in its different levels; the relationship between the member and its group; the *shtëpia*-group as the smallest eligible unit in terms of social obligations; brotherhood, and the double role of group and female. Chapter III built on Weber's Old Protestant Capitalist Spirit is therefore called the Albanian "Old Spirit". This chapter focuses on such traditional customs as *nderi, besa, mikpritja, and beja,* (among which is also *gjakmarrja* that for its importance in this essay will be described and analyzed in the Chapter IV). All these customs were deeply embedded in Albanian culture as long as they were an unquestioned part of life. However, my goal is to describe and analyze their functions and roles in the social Albanian web-obligation, which in full harmony with the social network seem to have made possible a self-governance system. There is a detailed description and analysis of the social phenomenon of *gjakmarrja* and its rituals in the Chapter IV Between Killing and Reconciliation that explains the regulator role in keeping social cohesion. Chapter V The Anthropology of *Gjakmarrja* aims at further analyzing and explaining the social-cultural environment of gjakmarrja, its place and its role in Albanian tradition. If this were the last chapter, this essay would not intention of contrasting what gjakmarrja traditionally was with what is currently known as *gjakmarrja*. This contrast was what initiated my study. Therefore, there is also an epilogue in which I draw more general conclusions and what might be helpful for further cultural study of Albania and Albanians.

# II

## THE TRADITIONAL SOCIAL STRUCTURE

Durham, in her book *High Albania* noticed that the tribe (*fis*) "has been both...[the Albanian high-landers'] strength and their weakness" (p, 20). I consider this as a key in explaining *gjakmarrja*. Before explaining the double role of this group, I have to clarify the boundaries of it. What Durham or Hasluck called tribe, or other scholars called clan, is known as *familja* (family) by the Kanun. On the page 14, article 18, (The Code of LD) the definition of family (*familja*) is given as "... a group of human beings live under the same roof...". In article 19 is stated, "[t]he family consists of the people of the house" (p, 19). In fact, the terms clan, tribe, or *njerëzit e shtëpisë* (people of the house) biologically mean the same extended group of people related by blood or marriage. What the Kanun calls *familja* (family) or *njerëzit e shtëpisë (people of the house)* was also the above group of people, but sharing the same *kulla* (a stone dwelling). At this point, this *shtëpia-* group gains responsibility for its members and might be considered (in terms of the obligations) as an extended family. Thus, the group of *njerëzit e shtëpisë* was a tribe or clan in biological terms but it appeared as a/n [extended] family in terms of responsibility.

The highlanders had strong restriction and penalties for marriages or illegal sexual intercourses within of the group called *njerëzit e shtëpisë*. On the other side, considering sexual intercourses among them as *turp* (dishonor) and incestuous showing they had extended the biological boundaries of the parental family. Thus, the *shtëpia*-group was considered family not only in terms of obligations but also in terms of strong sexual restrictions within *shtëpia*-group. The last thing to be added is that their *familja*, for various reasons, had different structure. In this essay, however, I will continue using the term *shtëpia*-group as the smallest eligible unit, subject to inter and intra obligations. For analogy, it should be said that the *shtëpia*-group was the strength and the weakness of the highlanders.

In this sense, the largest unit would be the highlanders' community that appeared as a network of social affiliations starting with *shtëpia*-group and continuing to other community levels as brotherhoods (*vllazni*-brothers) and banners (*flamurë*-flags). They used to share the same territory, and in terms of obligations and rights, worked at different levels of an extended family. Regardless of the fact that the people affiliated with these levels did not live under the same roof, the marriage interchanges in vllazni (brotherhood) were always restricted and those inside the banner system were not preferred. Hasluck said, "These communities consisted in the narrower sense of the family and in the wider sense of the tribe. If a person was injured, the family in most cases, and tribe in a few cases, by the law of self-government punished the wrongdoer (p, 219).

There was a web of obligations on different levels. Level one: Inside the *shtëpia*-group all the members appeared equally in their rights and obligations to the group; there were strong restrictions of the female members. It is crucial to understand that the dominant feature is in the relationship between the individual (the member) and the group. The relationship between members of the same group was also affected by the idea of the power of the group. However, even the equality, reciprocity, and solidarity were essential features of the traditional Albanian community, there was nothing fake among the members of the same group: Inside their groups as in most communities they had the duality of love and hatred, agreements and quarrels, jealousy and sometimes murders. To married the widow of the killed brother was not only an old custom, but also a reason for murders within family.

Outside the *shtëpia*-group, any of its members was not an individual but a representative of the group; the group was responsible for the obligations created by any of its member. The shtëpia-group might expand through establishing new alliances that were once established between two members belonging to different groups and then the alliance expanded to both groups. Level two: any shtëpia-group, as the only eligible subject in terms of the obligations, also held the power to act as an equal group within the community. In this respect, when the representatives of two different groups interacted, this was considered as an inter-group-action; every group was responsible for its member representatives. On the other side, when the problem extended outside the community (banner or village), then the entire community acted responsible for all the members; at this point, the ties between member and the *shtëpia*-group remained formal. Level three: This was the nation-level. All Albanians regardless of age, religion, and geographical location considered themselves as brothers (vëllezër) presuming they had the same enemies.

In this chapter I will mostly focus on the dynamics of the relationship between a member and the group. On the other side, I will describe the different groups of brotherhood as groups of mutually obligated alliances. Also, parts of this chapter explain the dual meaning of the group and the dual role of the Albanian female.

## THE MEMBER AS THE GROUP REPRESENTATIVE

Rather than personal identity, being only a representative of the group, the individual funcioned with the identity of the group. Thus, a person from the village of Dukagjin, called *Pal Zefi* (*Pal*-the first name, *Zefi*-the last name and Dukagjini-the banner) was *Pal* only at home. Otherwise, he was a *Zef-aj* (one of the Zefs) or Pal i Zefëve outside his shtëpia-group. He was also a Dukagjinas ouside his banner. Thus, any individual, as a representative held different identities in inter-group-actions that, however, were always related to the identity of the extended groups. Also, any individual, included in at least one group, (by birth, blood, marriage, or spiritual relationship) held full knowledge for the set of the rights and obligations both within and between groups. There were only two choices: To know and follow the rules and power of the group (represented by the chief), or to leave. On the other side, the membership of at least one group obligated the member to all other extended groups, where its group was linked in order to survive. Thus, being by birth a member of a parental family forced the member to be included (as part of its *shtëpia*-group) to the group of brotherhood and the group of banner. In this sense, all were, on various levels, extended forms of the family-group. Thus, the complex of rights and duties unfolded into the social environment of the shtëpia-group that extended to the others totally dominated by the chief-form in all levels. Since this essay is primarily interested in the obligations between the group and its representatives, I will say that the entire system worked hard on all levels to "repair" the holes-obligations of a/n endless, unlimited, and complicated web-obligation.

It seems that the scheme of intra-obligations appeared as a miniature of the biggest scheme: A (male) member with equal rights inside the group (with some restrictions but illegible to create obligations outside its group) and a group that would act fully responsible to the obligations created by anyone of its individual members. In other words, the obligations created by a member were considered as obligations of the entire group; any (male) member had the same probability to be picked based on the common group consent to fulfill group obligations. In these circumstances a member would act only as a representative of his own *shtëpia*-group or to others of extended levels.

The *shtëpia*-group and not the individual was the smallest link that held full power during juridical and social transactions. This feature stands in sharp contrast to the constitutional right of the individual who, by most modern constitutions, after the age of eighteen holds full juridical ability for social and financial transactions being found fully responsible for the transactions. Thus, as the Kanun says under The Rights and the Obligations of the Members of the Household (p, 18) the members of the *shtëpia*-group equally shared the full right of living and being honored, but only partially the right of individually acts outside *kulla*. The Kanun said, "[T] hey may not go to work for someone else without the permission of the head of the house" (p, 18) and "... may not sell or buy or exchange anything"(p, 18). Article 25 also said that, the members of the household "... may give guarantees... only to the value of their weapons, as these are their own property" (p, 18). This shows that the property of the members belonged to the *shtëpia*-group and the member held the right to take actions only for his own individual property.

On the other hand, the transactions between the banner (village) and any member as individual had two different sides. Once, the banner-group and individual had the same working scheme if the case included two different banners. Then, any individual was a representative of his banner and the banner was found (in some degrees) responsible to discharge the obligations created by its own members. On the other side, if it was an intra- banner case, the relationship between the banner (represented by the group of elders *–pleqtë* or the meeting of the banner *–fshatçe*) and the individual were almost infantile. In this second case, the banner-group called the individual only as a witness within his own individual case. Otherwise, any other transaction between banner and individual was a transaction between the banner and the member's group (usually the shtëpia-group). Even if the member appeared to individually act, he never represented just himself. In every case, the verdict given to him was an obligatory verdict to the entire group.

## THE SHTËPIA - GROUP

The strength of the highlander was to the *shtëpia*-group. This group was usually comprised of "as many as 20 persons" living under the same roof, all in the patrilineal descent line (Hasluck, M. pp: 25; 29). Father, mother, unmarried daughters, and sons with their brides, as well as grandchildren and the parents of the father, his widow or unmarried sisters, the single or widower brother- all shared the same shelter, ate meals and worked together sharing the results of their labors.

Everybody in the *shtëpia-group* used the same last name. It was not unusual for this surname to be the name of their father or grandfather. In other words, the *shtëpia-*group was considered as a nucleus made by members equal in their intra group rights and obligations. This status, as we have stressed above, did not always hold true for a female group member. I will further explain the dual role of an Albanian female to another part of the essay.

This group's chief was called *i zoti i shtëpisë- the god of the house* (the master of the house). He had the full power to lead his group. "The master's rule over his household was absolute and extended to every aspect of its life" (Hasluck, M. p,35). The master of the house was usually chosen based on common consent. According to the *Kanun*, " if the eldest of the family [did] not possess those qualities which were required to fulfill this office properly, then- [again] on the basis of common consent-another member of the household was chosen, who was wiser, more intelligent, and more careful. The head of the house may also be an unmarried man" (The Code of LD. p, 14.).

The *shtëpia-group* appeared as a strong unit with clear rights, obligations, and goals. The aim of the family was, "...to increase their number by means of marriage" and "to develop the physical, emotional, and intellectual state of its members" (The Code of LD. p, 14). Thus, an Albanian highlander member of the *shtëpia-*group held multiple power: His power represented the entity power. The *shtëpia-*group should have played a prominent role in the surviving struggle against human enemies, beasts, and the environment. Using the working power of the entire *shtëpia-group* instead of just one individual, it should have been an appreciated positive factor for survival of the highlanders who lived in a very difficult physical environment with little means securing a living and in a very mountainous area where even *kulla* from *kulla* were within a few minutes of walking. The Albanian highlanders, according to the travelers and scholars, used to live in a dual pastoral agricultural environment. People made their living mostly by raising livestock and cultivating maize. Females cooked, wove their clothes and rugs, and took care of the children and elders in the house. Thus, strong communities were not only a perceived cultural need was not only a need, but also a necessity for physically surviving.

## THE DUAL ROLE OF GROUP

Since a strong community was cultural need and a necessity for physically surviving, it is understandable that the matter of fulfilling group obligations should have been a key for keeping the group strong. Besides being fully responsible in discharging the individual intra obligations, generally, by addressing the *Kanun*, all the members of the *shtëpia*-group equally shared the same responsibility to discharge their group (inter) obligations. This equality stems from the relationship between the member and his group. Thus, it did not matter who created the obligation; since the obligation belonged to the entire group, any member of the group was equally responsible. As always, the representative was picked by common consent. The children and females had the right to be restricted. However, it was not unusual for females or children to voluntarily became involved in such inter-group cases, at least to any *gjakmarrja* case.

In these terms, it seems beyond a doubt that the *shtëpia*-group as the most important link of the web-obligation was at the same time the weakest point to the Albanian highlanders. Hasluck brings different reasons about why brothers might decide to live separately; the common reasons were the members' quarrels during the long winter time (p, 51). In such cases, a punishment (for example a food deprivation) could be given to the member by the master of the house (The Code of LD. p, 15). However, I believe that the biggest reason to point to the *shtëpia*-group as the highlanders' weakness comes from the responsibility of the *shtëpia*-group fulfilling the obligations of all its members. It seems that so many males living under the same roof increased the probability of being obligated for each member within the group, which, in other words might be "translated" as more blood to be "borrowed".

The member appeared in his or her own identity only in intra *shtëpia*-group cases. The *Kanun* deeply affected the life of this group also. Thus, the rules of marriage, wedding, the obligations of groom and bride to each other and between them and other members of their respective kinfolks were outlined by the *Kanun* strictly and in full details (pp, 21-23). Marriage for love was never mentioned in the *Kanun*. It has been said that to love husband and respect the members of his family were a wife's duty, but this was always in terms of life after the marriage. With respect to this, it was also a groom's duty to love his bride and to respect her kinship. Divorce, even if it could happen was never favorable. Sexual intercourse out of marriage was considered a shame not only for the couple but for their kinships groups, too. Extreme punishment was given to such a couple under the *Kanun*. The children born out of wedlock were considered as a misfortune and fatalities. Out of wedlock pregnancies always ended with murdering both the pregnant female and the baby. In other words, all of above complicated the life of highlanders bringing new opportunities for quarrels, obligations, and deaths.

As Durham said, "...the "family" (for the highlander) was entity; the individual had no separate existence" (p, 35). As we already pointed any member outside the group could act only as a representative of it. On the other hand, as a rule, community (even though in different levels) was always responsible for the obligations created by its members. "If a person was injured, the family in most cases, and tribe in a few cases, by the law of self-government punished the wrongdoer" (Hasluck, M. p, 219).

The *Kanun* stated that, "The head of the house is responsible for any damage committed by a member of his household" (p, 18). There were cases that the community by itself decided to discharge its obligation by dismissing or killing its member (male or female), but this would happen only in a case where ethics was a strong issue.

Thus, the out of the wedlock pregnancy was one of the examples. Since such pregnancies were considered as *turp* (shame) that should be cleansed, the killing of the pregnant woman caused no further group obligation. In another case, a brother has killed his younger brother because the last one, for a reward from government, had given their *miku* up. This was called *të presësh mikun në besë* (betrayed the guest) and was considered a big shame that only blood would cleanse it (Durham, E. p, 172). After the killing within the group, no further obligations to the guest's group were recorded. The most frequent case traditionally known was when a female was accused of adultery said to bring home the *faqja e zezë* (the black cheek) for had an illegal affair or sex. Then her father or her brother would kill her to keep the honor of their *shtëpia*-group. In this case they were set free from resolving the obligation that she created between her father's and brother's *shtëpia*-group and her husband's group.

The same case would apply to a single female. Her father and her brother, *për të shpëtuar nderin* (to save face), would kill her for her having a love affair. This was a case with a strong ethical background. If they did not take any action, the *shtëpia*-group would then face shame even in front of the brotherhood or the banner. Thus, her *shtëpia*-group seems obligated to its extended groups for saving honor. In such cases both of the lovers would be caught and killed. By the *Kanun*, the lover's group had no right to apply *gjakmarrja* for its killed member, because he created trouble for himself and for the both of the groups. Thus, the male member death set his group free of any additional obligations. However, such case might be one that started a long blood feud.

This could happen in any case were the victim's group was not totally convinced of legitimacy of what happened. It was not rare that the family by itself, just in case, gave to the daughter a cartridge in her dowry. This cartridge was given to the groom transferring to him the legal right of killing her if she was not found to be avirgin on the first night of marriage. No further obligations were recorded from both sides in such case.

## BROTHERHOOD

The brotherhood-groups show that *shtëpia*-group support was not always sufficient for its individual members. In cases of war the highlanders would have been in strong need for new alliances. However, sentiments and values had a key role in creating a situation of brotherhood by choice. Another time, this group was a result of the reconciliation between two of the groups.

## VLLAZNIA- SEPARATED BROTHERS

The blood patrilineal affiliations *vllaznia* (separated brothers) might be considered as natural alliance groups since they are naturally affiliated by agnates. The Kanun said that *vllaznia* (separated brothers) relates to brothers separated from the same house. We have to clarify this point: Brothers separated from the same house means brothers that lived in the same house during previous generations. In other words, *vllaznia* usually included all agnates but where some of the cognates were not prohibited. However, agnates kept special relationship among themselves. In terms of being an extended family they might have been involved in the same social obligations within their brotherhood; which is not always true for any of the other cognate. Highlanders involved in a *vllaznia* relationship had full knowledge of their blood relationship level; they went to each other on occasions of marriage, death, or other social events, and they might exchange gifts during traditional or religion holidays. At this level, even though agnates were prohibited from exchanging marriages; they were usually free of *gjakmarrja* obligations.

## VLLAMI- BROTHER BY CHOICE

The highlanders had also developed the blood brotherhood. In what is called "blood brotherhood", the members of this group were not connected at all by blood. Instead, this group was developed in cases of a strong need for agreement of trust or cooperation between two groups behind male with no blood relationship. In order to legitimate the agreement, two from their representatives should swear the *besa* (the code of honor) and might decide to drink blood from each other's bodies. After drinking each other's blood they were considered biological siblings and this was accepted by everybody in their respective *shtëpia*-groups each considering the other group at the same level as a *vllaznia*- group. I must add here that in the case of blood brotherhood *shtëpitë e vllamëve* (the houses of the brothers by choice) continued living separately but with close relationship ties. Exchange marriages in blood brotherhood were, however, prohibited (Durham, E. p, 24). I doubt this rule remained static or was not changing. I have heard of marriage arrangements in blood brotherhood just at the moment before the drinking of the blood took place. In such case the marriage was accepted as another reason for the making of a the new alliance stronger.

There were also restrictions between the two groups in terms of mutual obligations. Thus, *vllami* might be a member of the team that would take blood in account of such brother by choice, but he cannot be the *gjaks* ( killer) (Hasluck, M. p, 221). Otherwise, a new branch of the *gjakmarrja* obligation would be transferred to his own group. In other words, if *gjakmarrja* occurred to his *vllamë* family, the *Kanun did not obligate the vllami*, but he would be accepted as involved in such an obligation, if he wanted to show his loyalty and friendship to his *vllami*-group. The *vllami* was a very important mutual institution in war, peace, or life. The blood brotherhood meant peace, friendship, *besë,* help, alliances, and increased power among the Albanian highlanders.

## KUMBARA - THE SPIRITUAL BROTHERHOOD

Other friendship alliances were established based on ceremonies of cutting hair, baptism, and marriage. "The woman that assisted the cut of the umbilical cord at the birth of an infant" might have been an eligible case for spiritual connections (Durham, E. p, 25). Those are the only alliances made regardless of gender. The group of the *kumbara* (the godmother) or *kumbari* (the godfather) was considered as cognates. They were always respected. On the other side, Durham noticed that, a forbidden marriage existed not only in blood relations on "the male side, but [also] into spiritual relationships. "They (the highlanders) do not consider as intermarriageable the relationship with godfather of baptism and the godfather of hair" (p, 23). They were also denied from the obligation of gjakmarrja (Hasluck, M. p, 221). In the paragraph 39, page 24 of entitled the *Kanun*, to the "Obstacles to Marriage" it is stated that, "There must be no spiritual relationship [between the young man and woman] due to: 1)baptism [i.e. through godparents]; 2) marriage; 3) cutting the hair [to establish a special formal relationship of close friendship]; and 4) there must be no relationship of blood-brotherhood [established between two young men, who swear brotherhood by each sucking a little blood from the cut finger of the other].

## THE DUAL ROLE OF FEMALE

To clarify from what was said above the *Kanun* enforced gender discrimination. As Durham has noticed, "[t]he birth of a daughter [was]...considered a misfortune" (p, 37). On the other side, even though the *Kanun* said that, "Soul by soul, all are equal to God" (p, 130) a woman, in general, possessed fewer rights that even a newborn male. She was considered as "a sack, made to endure as long as she lives in her husband's house" (The Code of LD. p, 38). It was also known that a female group member had no right for inheritance. On the other hand, every man had the right to consider his wife as his own property, even if that "the husband does not have the right over the life of his wife" (p, 44). Only in flagrant cases of adultery, did a husband have the right to kill his wife, but this might happen only in case of his getting her group's permission. Otherwise he owed her blood to her group. In other cases, the obligation of killing belonged to her family. By the *Kanun*, a woman, however, was forbidden to hold weapons (p, 38). The *Kanun* prohibited the female from being picked for fulfilling of any social obligations of the group. It was her duty to fulfill the social obligations occurred to her as a daughter, wife, and mother.

On the other side, a female's position was supported by the *Kanun* in terms of protecting her right to have a family, " a) Legal marriage, approved by the Faith and the *Kanun* of Lekë; b) Keeping a woman outside of marriage, against the Faith and the *Kanun* of Lekë; c) Abducting a woman or girl, in opposition to the Faith and the *Kanun*; d) trial marriage, against the faith and the *Kanun*" (p, 20). In traditional folk songs, tales, and ballads a highlander female is pictured as beautiful, with the highest human values, and especially as very loyal to her brother and husband. *Rozafa, Nora, and Shota* are some of the names of women highly evaluated from the highlanders' society. There are also cases showing that highlander females did bear weapons and, in times of male shortages they avenged the father, the brother, or the husband. No sanctions were then recorded against them. It is a matter of fact that the *Kanun* prohibited or restricted females, but in special cases there were no sanctions against them.

Even though that the highlanders' society sanctioned the treatment of women as cattle (Broughton, J. C. p, 129) the *Kanun* allowed the change of her status if she acted as a man discharging any blood obligation, or if she had sworn to remain a virgin. Thus, Hasluck tells about Emin, the virgin of Orenjë in Çermenikë that "avenged her father" (p, 223). If the girl had sworn to remain a virgin, she usually would never get married. "In Maltsia e Madhe a girl who has sworn virginity- "an Albanian virgin"- can, if her father left no son, inherit land and work it. At her death it goes to her father's nearest heir male. These women as a rule used to wear male clothes and may carry arms" (Durham, E. p, 38) and were admitted by society to fulfill the obligation of a man in exchange for giving her all the rights of a male member. If the girl who sworn virginity decided to get married she could marry only her "first husband"- the man to whom, as a rule, she was sold by her family even before her birth. In any other case, her family lost face if she married another person. The friendship was broken and the right and obligation of the *gjakmarrja* came into play.

I would add that the dual role of female in the network supports the idea that a woman was always restricted and rejected in favor of keeping the obligations of the group short. Her discrimination, however, do not question the reciprocity and equality principles, to which it was built the entire social structure of the Albanian highlanders. Instead, the female was always an exception to the rule. I believe that the strong restrictions on female rights and obligations were always in favor of supporting the strength of the group.

As a summary for this chapter, in terms of Emile Durkheim, the highlanders' society would be described as a pre-agricultural society, where the social cohesion was based upon the likeness and similarities among individuals and largely dependent on common rituals and routines. Thus, the mechanical solidarity, as the solidarity of the members of a community where every individual performs the same or nearly the same tasks as all others within community, makes all individuals the same responsible and even equal for the obligations to and for the community; the female is a exception to the rule.

Additionally, the Albanian highlanders' network had different links, where the shtëpia-group, in terms of obligations, appeared as the strongest and weakest point: the strongest- because the individual power was multiplied by the group power; the weakest- because any member of the group was the same responsible to all the group obligations. Even though the obligations were created in different situations they might be entirely transferred to any member. All other groups as brotherhood, banner, and even the entire nation worked as an extended family. All individuals equally shared their rights of living, being honored, and with some restrictions, the right of creating obligations. A member always acted as a representative of its group. Its obligations were considered as the entire group's obligations. Any member within the group had the same possibility to be picked based on common consent as the representative of its group in order to fulfill the group's obligations. A dual role for female was recorded. A set of customs, beliefs, rituals, and institutions were built at this network where the obligations remained the responsibility of the group and all members, who shared the same identity belonged to the group.

# III

## THE ALBANIAN "OLD SPIRIT"

Any Albanian highlander asked why he might kill another, would answer, "For [the sake of the] honor". Among social duties for the Albanian highlander, the saving face (*faqja e bardhë*- white cheek) had a special importance. *Nderi* (honor) remained the kernel of the Albanian old spirit. In this chapter I will focus on the highlanders' *nderi* (honor) not only as a human virtue, but also as an essential feature of the relationship between the individual and group. Honor was considered as epitome of a set of human values: wisdom, balance, honesty, respect, friendship, courage, and self-dominance. Honor was also the respect given to promise, agreement, and obligation. A full set of social transactions as *besa* (the code of honor), *mikpritja* (hospitality), *beja* (oath), and *gjakmarrja* as type of the blood feud were part of the same social system; the "engine" of which was called *nderi* (honor). The social transactions, on one side, depended on certain situations, were considered as obligatory, and on the other side, held an institutional power developing further rights and obligations to the Albanian highlanders and their respective groups. I would add that they were culturally involved in the basic daily life of the highlanders.

## NDERI (HONOR)

Any good Albanian should first of all be an honored man. It seems that an Albanian highlander had to take different social actions maintaining the (highest) level of honor; in case of honor being jeopardized, further social actions had to be taken.

## FREE TO BE HONORED

The highlanders have a greeting that is not in use to others. They still say, *"A je burrë?"* (Are you a man?) instead of "How are you". The word *burrë* is used also in the expression "Bëhu burrë" (Be a man). To express high values of female, the highlanders call her *burrneshë* (*burrë*+ the prefix *–neshë*). (It is the same rule that make widower from widow but in Albanian language the female comes from the masculine gender). This is not what might be apparently thought: A female brought to the quality of a male. Instead, the word burrë (male, man) in certain conditions is used for an honorable man. Thus, there is another word that expresses also the value: *Burrni* ( *Burr(ë)*+ *ni),* which is the qualification of the situation that comes after the situation "To be a man" is succeeded. The antonym of the word *burrni* in the Albanian language is *shburrni*. In analogy with other Albanian words with the suffix "sh", the *shburrni* is the situation described as losing *burrni*. The Kanun said, "Je i lir me mbajtë burrnin t"ande; je i lir me u shburrnue- You are free to hold your honor, you are free to get the shame*(p, 115). Then, another article continued, "Kanuja thote: Ftyrën e vrugnueme ne daç laje, në daç zezoje edhe ma.- The Kanun says: Wash the dirty from your face if you prefer , or if you prefer, make it blacker" (p, 115). There are some conclusions that can be drown from the above statement: One, the words *burrë and burrni* appeared as homonymous of honored man ( njeri i nderuar) and honor (*nderi*); two, the word *burrneshë* was used to show the quality of a honored female ( who, however, as I shall explain, to be a honored member had to go through the male's identity); and three, the highlander had a strong interest (Are you a [honored] man?) to the *nderi* quality.

It seems that every Albanian highlander enjoyed the right to be honored (You are free to keep your (burrnia) honor...). On the Book Eight (Honor), Chapter Seventeen, article 593, it is said, " The Kanun of the Albanian mountains does not make any distinction between man and man. 'Soul for soul, all are equal before God'." (The Code of LD. p, 130). Also, as we will see under the *mikpritja* (hospitality) explanation, the hospitality was an institution that legitimated the right of the honor (the guest with the right to be honored; the host that would be honored upon the discharging the obligation of honoring the guest).

To fully understand the Albanian honor (*të qënit faqebardhë*- being with a white cheek), one must understand that to the highlander, honor was considered more important that life by itself. The Kanun said, "The man who has been dishonored is considered dead" (The Code of LD. p, 130). Social death was very tragic, because the dishonored person kept both of the qualities (dead and dishonored) for the rest of his life. In fact, since the highlanders believed in life after death, the life of being dishonored was considered an eternal one. Furthermore, *faqja e zezë* - the black cheek (dirty) was transmitted to the group. The biological death of a dishonored man, even if it might save some of the formal treatments of a death occasion, also held the elements of a strong public disappointment. Thus, on some occasions, people, as a social tacit sanction, refused to attend the ceremony of mourning and burial of the dead. It was not rare that during the process of mourning the lamenting person publicly sang the circumstances of losing face-a fact that was considered very tragic, shameful, and never forgotten. As people were afraid, that losing face would be transmitted from the father to the sons and from the sons to their sons' sons up to seven generations. There are known cases that an entire group have moved out from the banner and have changed the last name in order to get a new identity that was not only highly desirable but also a necessity for normal life of the group.

Honor never remained a personal quality. As part of the group identity, *nderi* was a transferable quality from one generation to another. However, the *nderi* or *turpi* were always personally cared for and all members were equal responsible for saving the honor. A person with a good name (*njeri me emër të mirë*)- as a person with a good reputation was called-had many chances for turning into a person with a bad name (*njeri me emër te keq*)- as a person with bad reputation was called. Since any daily action could lead to a case of losing honor, it seems that losing the "good name" was a daily fear of Albanian highlander. Thus, on one hand the Albanian man faced biological death (from which, related to the Albanian set of values, one should never afraid). On the other hand, he feared the social death: losing honor, which was considered worse than real death.

Social death was not only an ethical issue. At the same time, social sanctions against a dishonored man were followed by juridical sanctions. First of all, a member from a dishonored clan usually lost social access. Thus, no one would want to be married to a member from a dishonored group. Second, the contest of such witness was never treated as eligible. Third, the social stigma would follow a dishonored member for the rest of the life. People avoided even talking to them (my grandma used to say, "Pity on them for what they have put upon themselves -Të mjerët ata cfarë i bënë vehtes!). Usually they were not welcomed at social occasions. If it happen to be there, they had to handle the embarrassment of having a cup of coffee only half filled, which, would be given under the knee to any of them, "...reminding him of his disgrace. "[Such member]... was often mocked openly" (Hasluck, M. p, 232). In other words, as a conclusion based on the study of the Kanun, it seems clear that the honor status was the status of that one individual, the group of whom was free from any social obligation.

## THE OBLIGATION OF BEING HONORED

It should be understood that the highlanders' society was designed as the community of equal, honored men. They had a right to be honored; they held the right to get shame. However, there were social and juridical sanctions against them, who were considered dishonored. To be honored was a social obligation. In this part I will focus on the cases of making a man dishonored. The Kanun, in its 615 act (pp: 131-132) said, "[A] man is considered dishonored:

- If someone calls him a liar in front of a group of men;
- If someone spits at him, threatens him, pushes him, or strikes him;
- If someone reneges on his promise of mediation or in his pledged word;
- If his wife is insulted or if she runs off with someone;
- If someone takes the weapons he carries on his shoulder or in his belt;
- If someone violates his hospitality, insulting his friend

or his worker;

- If someone breaks into his house, his sheepfold, his silo, or his milk-shed in his courtyard;
- If someone does not repay a debt or obligation;
- If someone removes the cover of a cooking pot in his hearth;
- If someone dips a morsel of food before the guest, the guest is dishonored;
- If someone disgraces the table in the presence of a guest, after the master of the house has had the dinner utensils removed".

Based on the above cases, a man (and also his group) could be dishonored based only on eligible reasons. A man would be dishonored when he directly violates his social obligations (the cases with numbers 3, 6, and 8). For all other cases, he would also be dishonored, even though it seems he does not initiate the rule violation. This is clearly shown on the cases number 1, 2, 4, 5, 7, 9, 10, and 11. Thus, if a man (number 9) removes the cover of a cooking pot in somebody else's earth (home), why does dishonor remain with the host? I would say that in these cases social obligation is still an issue.

As in the cases number 3, 6, and 8, a wrong action would clearly conflict with the social obligation, to all of the other cases, being passive would also be a violation of a social obligation: the obligation of keeping honor. The host was dishonored upon the violation of the obligation for being honored. The shame remained with the host until he took further actions to regain his honor again. In the best case he had to punish the guilty guest. The punishment was also an obligation that directly came from the violation of the obligation of being honored. I also believe that this is a case in the violation of hospitality, which was also considered sacred. At the same situation, the host was responsible for the guest during the first twenty-four hours after the guest left the house. The reason seems not to be clear, but I think it related to the magic power of bread. Since hospitality and bread (*bukë, kripë dhe zemer*- bread, salt, and heart: The host's greeting to the guest) were the responsibility of the host, the punishment of the violator became a social obligation of the host.

Based on reciprocity (The Albanians still say, "Do not do to others what you do not wish happening to you. - *Mos i bëj tjetrit atë, që s'të pëlqen të ta bëjnë ty.*) and self-governing rule, I would say that the punishment of a wrongdoer should have also been the social obligation for any member. Thus, a reason could be that someone decided to call another a "liar" (The case 1). Who was dishonored? Who was guilty? Since the first action happened in an unknown situation, guilt and dishonor remains with the man that is publicly evaluated as such. (Guilty until proven innocent: He is called a liar and until he proves his innocence, he remains a dishonored man). By the *Kanun*, a "liar" was allowed to take further actions to get his honor back. Moreover, by the *Kanun*, the "liar" was forced into further social actions; otherwise his claim for being honored would be rejected and he would be finally treated as dishonored. In other words, he will be considered as socially dead, which is also the status of the individual that violates social obligations. This analysis clearly shows that honor was a social obligation, the braking up of which, would bring into play different social sanctions.

Thus, the honored man was considered any individual who promised to fulfill the group social obligations until he had a violation case. This was a social credit that any member received in advance by the community upon the quality of being an equal member. On these terms the community was the group of the honored men. Honor was the status that the representatives of the group received from the group that already held this quality fulfilling its social obligations as an entity. In other words, the honor of the group as part of the group identity was reflected and multiplied to all its members (which was also true in the case of shame). The group also offered this status to anyone else upon a promise of discharging any possible obligation of the group. I will continue to develop this idea under the *miku* (guest) category.

I think that the Albanian community for different reasons was built to work as a *perpetual mobile*. Equality, solidarity, and reciprocity seem that create a favorable environment for a successive culture based on self-governance. The highlanders' network offers an affiliated model centered and dependant not on the individual, but the *shtëpia*-group as being the smallest social unit to appear with its own social identity and the full juridical ability of acting and having responsibility during mutual inter-group-transactions. The individual, as the representative of the group was forced to interact in the web-obligation of the society in a well-defined direction, determined by the position and interest of the group.

The *Kanun* said, "You are free to keep your honor..." (p, 115) and we call it as the right to be honored. The Kanun also said, "... You are free to get the shame" (p, 115) and it seems that a highlander would also enjoy the right to get shame, but then, in page 130, article 595 the Kanun said, "...if you prefer, wash your dirty face" continuing in the article 597, "[a]n offense to honor is never forgiven" (p, 130). In this part I will elaborate the idea that the right to be honored was in fact given as a social credit in advance of the tacit promise of the member to fulfill the obligations of/to the group. To keep the honorable status a highlander was supposed to go through a set of obligated transactions, institutions, and sanctions. The superstructure of this society was developed in such way as to self-control its social cohesion. It seems that there were not many choices left: To go through an obligated transactions, to respect the obligated institutions, and to use the obligated sanctions in order to remain honored. By the *Kanun*, the highlanders were always forced to face some obligated institutions as *miku* ( guest) and *vllami* ( brother by choice) that would result from getting into some obligated transactions as *mikpritja* - to welcome the guest (hospitality) and *besa* ( code of honor) as ways of gaining social control through new alliances.

## MIKPRITJA ( HOSPITALITY)

If there were any part of the Albanian tradition that even today continuously makes the highlanders proud, no doubt it would be *mikpritja: mik*- guest, *pritja*- waiting (hospitality). The *Kanun* said, "If a guest enters your house, even though he may be in blood with you, you must say to him, "Welcome!" (p, 134). On the other hand, it has been said, "The house of the Albanian belongs to God and the guest" (p, 132) giving the "God" status to the guest. It seems that hospitality was one of the most important transactions for a highlander in terms of new alliances and honor. Since *miku* (the guest) was considered a very important institution appearing with a complex of rights and obligations, the most important obligation was the respect of this institution. Thus, "the *Kanun* demands that a guest should be accompanied both lest he be the victim of some wicked act and lest he harm someone while under your protection" (The Code of LD. p, 134). The host was always found responsible for his guest's honor and for his guest's actions.

In case of violated hospitality, the Kanun gives only a choice of two paths for the host: "[potential] ruin or dishonor" (p, 136). Any offence but an offence made against a guest can be pardoned. We already discussed the case of the killing of a brother for the sake of hospitality. The answer is also given by the *Kanun*, "If you do not avenge the murder of your guest...you may not participate in meetings of honorable men, because you remain dishonored for the rest of your life" (p, 136). On the other hand, an Albanian knew how to forgive, he would forget any act that might damage his own personal interests, but he could not compromise on matters concerning honor. In other words, the *miku* institution that brought honor and new alliance, also brought new obligation; the failure to fulfill this was a new threat to the losing of honor to the guest and his group.

## BESA- MUTUAL SOCIAL AGREEMENT

When a highlander greets another *"A je burrë?"* (Are you a man?) the answer usually comes as *"Po, besa, burrë i fortë"* (Yes, a promise, [I am] a strong man). It seems that the translation of *besa* is also difficult. It might be described as a form of promise or pledge. Since we explained that honor (*nderi*) was considered the kernel of the Albanian highlanders' life, I would prefer the translation "the code of honor". The Kanun said, *"...me dhanë besë është detyrë dhe burrni-* to give *besa* is a duty and honor" (p, 165). An old Albanian expression says, "An Albanian would slay his son for the sake of *besa"* (*Shqiptari kur jep fjalën therr edhe djalën*). In contrast, having a son is very desirable for highlanders. The idea is not that the Albanian could easily kill a son, but it implies that the violation of the *besa* remained out of question. However, the translation cannot give the social context of *besa* that brought at the same time honor, friendship, alliance, power and also a new set of obligations accompanied with a new threat of losing honor. After being given, *besa* was always sacred. Durham said, "The besa, once given, is inviolable; its power is terrible" (p, 171).

*Besa* was the act of any unwritten social mutual agreement of trust or cooperation. This could be an agreement for alliance between two male members from different groups, involving both groups in the agreement and all obligations coming from the agreement (obligations that were never questioned by both sides). It could be also between two members inside the group or between a member and the whole group. We already have described and explained the sworn (a form of *besa*) under the *vllami* and *miku* categories. A further explanation will be given in the Chapter 3 and relates to the reconciliation or the twenty-four-hour and thirty-day truce. However, *besa* remains a mutual agreement even in cases that was given as a promise. In this case, *besa* as a promise for social service was exchanged for the advanced social credit of honor.

From the well-known Albanian legends, I have chosen the one that shows the meanings of the *besa*: its magic, beauty, and tragic. This is the Legend of Doruntina. It tells about a mother, who let her daughter to be marry in a far away place upon the *besa* of her son bringing his sister to visit her mother any time the mother would miss the daughter. But later on the brother was killed. The mother cries, "Konstandin my son/ where is your *besa* you gave to me?...Your *besa* is wasted under the earth- *Kostandin djali im, ku është besa që më dhe? Besa jote humbur ndënë dhe...*". Suddenly, Doruntina comes. Very happy but surprised, the mother asks, "Who brought you here". Being far away, Doruntina had heard nothing about the death of her brother. Instead, having a very long ride back with her brother, with one horse, she said, "My brother, Konstandin". The mother cries, "There are three years that Kostandin is dead ...How come he's not yet wasted? What kept him alive even after his death". It was *besa*. Even though dead, the son could not rest in peace. He had to "survive" only for the sake of keeping the promise to his mother. He wanted to be remembered as an honored man even after death.

Ismail Kadare says that *besa* was not just a *parole d'honeur* to Albanians; instead the code of honor was deeply embedded in the highlanders' lives. After all, it had all the dimensions of a constitution. *Besa* was given in terms of making new friends and alliances, undertaking promises and legitimating different social transactions. Even theoretically, the violation of the *besa* was considered by any highlander as the biggest shame. Such very rare cases had heavy consequences, that would distract not only from the life of the *i pabesi-* (without faith) the person that dare to break *besa*, but sometimes to a whole banner (1981. p, 24).

We said that besa was a promise, pledge, agreement. At the same time *besa* was an obligation, the failure of which was a subject even of the *gjakmarrja*. Të premt' e mikut në besë (to kill the guest during the besa- to kill one during the time or place that he was still eligible for the guest-status; a status automatically accompanied with the host's promise for care and defense) was one of the worse precedents in the life of the highlander. In this sense, it must be said that besa as other traditional social institutions, held the dual role of being at the same time an agreement and an obligation. I am speculating that the highlanders' community was a community of men who had sworn *besa* in order to discharge their obligations. Failure was a catastrophe that frequently brought blood seriously questioning the social cohesion of the group and community.

We previously valuated *besa* as a form of sworn obligation. Another form of it would be the *beja* (oath). By the *Kanun*, an accused member upon proven guilty had the right to take further social transactions in order to clean their honor (The Code of LD. p, 122). One of these acts was called the *be-ja* (oath). The Kanun said,

- "Rancor does not extend beyond the oath.
- Swear, and the accusation goes no further.
- The oath washes away blood.
- Lost objects and lost blood are equal before the oath.
- Either the oath or the object" (p, 120).

Being accused, a member would take an oath (*be*) calling "upon God in testimony of the truth [and] to submit oneself to the weight of eternal punishment..." (The Code of LD. p, 120). The oath was always a mutual transaction: To hold legal power it would satisfy a need for clearance; it would be given by the suspect; and it would be admitted by the compurgator. Hasluck explains that in Mirditë "a verdict was already known before the taking of the oath" (p, 189). Thus, in case the suspect felt ready to take a oath and the compurgators did not believe him, they refused his invitation for them having a meal in his house meaning that they did not admit the oath. Hasluck also predict that the oath was "equally efficient as an instrument of social cohesion, biding the tribe when occasion arose to concerted action against crime within and danger without" (p, 164).

I believe that *besa* and *beja* are the oldest customs. They held a strong authority upon being publicly made. I also believe that the "oath upon God" should have been a latter arrangement. The stone that Kanun offered besides the Cross and Gospel as tokens of the oath, shows that *beja* belonged even to the times before

Christ. "The oath upon a 'rock', according to the Kanun, is one of the strongest and purest oaths known to Albanian of the mountains" (The Code of LD. p, 115). According to the Kanun, there were different oaths such as The Door-to-Door Oath, The Oath on the Head of One's Sons, and the Oath of Ignorance. (Again, contrasting with the modern constitutions, which do not admit the ignorance about the rule, the Kanun admits ignorance of the principle). After the oath in general was given, the accuser had no right to trouble the suspect any more. However, the accuser had the right of the proving any oath false. In such cases, the suspect would pay double the value of the damage to the accused and face all other sanctions as a dishonored man.

The biggest sanction was believed to come from the magical power of the *beja* based on the reciprocity principle. The oath was not considered as valuable and eligible if the suspect did not included in the sanction that he deserved in the case of his being a liar. Thus, one form of the oath was as, "If I lie may God kill me. If I tell the truth, may he forgive my sins" (Hasluck, M. p, 192). As strong as the oath was, it was designed to clear the suspect. In contrast, a natural death or other causality to the group's suspect that had taken the oath, were considered as a sign that the man was guilty. However, if the suspect was proven guilty, he automatically took a dishonorable status. Then, there were a set of sanctions imposed.

The ethical sanctions: Not talking, no invitations to social occasions, serving the coffee from under the knee, and in few words basically totally being ignored in public. The social sanctions: Refusing marriages, dismissing him as witness, and denying any social access in general. The ban, fire, destruction and execution were the punishments given by the village for those considered like very strong cases as killing a guest, a priest, someone of his own clan, or other cases with strong ethical backgrounds like killing a murderer during a truce, killing a brother to take the bride, killing a cousin to take his property, and permitting the malefactors of the Banner to enter to his home.

I believe that ethical and social sanctions including the ban, destruction, fire, and death penalty given to a dishonored man and his entire group were based on the principles of equality, reciprocity, and solidarity. This is an issue by itself, the explanation of which included in an essay about *gjakmarrja* would be not sufficient. However, only for illustration I will bring here one of the applications of the *Kanun* of *Lekë Dukagjini*. It is said,

*"Nikollë Gjokë Perndoka of Kaçinar, Mirditë, from the Banner of Diber, as a result of some quarrel he had with a fellow-villager, Nikollë Marku, shot his gun at the latter's door, putting three bullet holes into it. The case came before the Elders and, when they had taken the evidence, they handed down the following judgment:*

*The damaged door of the house of Nikollë Marku shall be taken and brought to the house of Nikollë Gjokë Perndoka, and the door of his house shall be brought to the house of Nikollë Marku.*

*The door that was shot and perforated with holes shall be placed in the house of the person who shot, and he shall be liable to heavy fines if he dares not only to change it, but also to plug the bullet holes for a period of fifteen years.*

Aside from this, he is also fined 500 *grosh*" (The Code of LD. p, 228).

The example would be fully interpreted only in the above terms. First, the damaged door should be changed with the other door. The fine of 500 groshbeans (I believe the Albanian money of that time) was considered as an insufficient payment. Thus, the act held three parts: 1. Changing doors: You will keep the door that you shot, the other one will have the door that is not damaged. 2. Repair of the damaged door was prohibited as a sign of remained shame to the person who shot the door: You wanted to dishonor someone, you deserve dishonor. 3. The person, who shot the door, was charged paying a fine: You try to dishonor someone and you have to pay for it.

In the Albanian context, the "dramatic" concern of this case was the decline of the honor of *Nikollë Marku*, whose door had been shot. The case has started only because *Nikollë Marku* and *Nikollë Gjoka* were considered with the equal right to be honored; this was based on the equality principle. The case also was an Elder's case only based on the solidarity with the one to whom the damage had occurred. The three parts of the verdict were based on the reciprocity principle: the exchange of the doors, the fine, and the obligation to keep the damaged door with the wholes for fifteen years. Based on the ethical issue, the justice, in favor to *Marku*, decided to prohibit the repair of the damaged door as a property of *Nikollë Gjoka*, who, in this case, was punished in order to return the lost honor to *Marku*.

# IV

## BETWEEN KILLING AND RECONCILIATION

*T*he **gjakmarrja** *grew beyond sentiments: It was not frustration, hatred, nor pleasure. It was not related only to the blood-boiling, murder, or only to the killer or victim. On the web-obligation, the* **gjakmarrja** *was the threat of the death penalty for them who took advantage to someone's guest, weapon, and female; it was at the same time the right and the obligation of one who was insulted, injured, or killed. I would refer to the* **gjakmarrja** *as one of the important regulators built to control the social cohesion in a quite simple system based on equality, reciprocity, solidarity, and self-governance. In a perpetual cycle of exchanges within and between generations* **gjakmarrja** *should be addressed as a sanction of the self controlled system where the own individual interest was totally affected by the interest of the group.*

### HONOR OR FATALITY?

The *gjakmarrja* might come into play in any case where the group honor would be extremely jeopardized by the killing of any member, or where a strong ethical background (violation of hospitality, weapons, or adultery) was the case. On the other side, the belief of killing for the sake of the honor was confirmed by the *Kanun*. Thus, it should be said that the killer's duty was not just taking blood from the enemies' side, but also to publicly show that the murder was for the sake of honor and only on purpose of it. Some very preciously rituals were required by the *Kanun* in this respect. The ritual of killing was designed even in details to express honor for the victim and group. Some customs as the turning of victim over on the back, placing the weapon near to the victim's head, attending (by the murderer) the mourning and burial ceremony, eating the meal of the dead (*drekën e të vdekurit*) strongly support the belief that killing was only for the sake of honor. The stealing of the personal properties (including the weapon) and the violation of the victim were prohibited and punished by the Kanun. "If [the gjaksi] commits such a dishonorable act, he incurs two blood-feuds" (The Code of LD. p, 164). Even though all these rituals and strict rules prove how deep the highlanders were involved in their beliefs and obligations of doing everything right and for the sake of honor, I would add that reading or hearing the *gjakmarrja* stories, rather than killing for honor one would have the impression that it was an "invisible" power that always pushed people to preciously follow rules and rituals of killing.

The *gjakmarrja* situation in Albanian language would be pronounced in different forms: më ka gjakun (he owns my blood), jemi në gjak (we are in blood), te marrësh gjak (to take blood). All these expressions give the superficial impression that there is a financial transaction between individual or groups involved into financial agreements and obligations: I will take the blood that you have borrowed from me. There is one single form used for both the groups: *të biesh në gjak*. Nothing is lost from the translation from the Albanian language into the English language "to fall in blood". Related to other expressions as *to fall in* love, *to fall apart*, *fall down* and so the list goes on, the fatality seems to start right from the linguistic meaning of the verb *bie* (fall), which, in both the languages, is used at the same form giving the impression that both the killer and victim were passively involved (fallen) in *gjakmarrja*. They seem to hold and share the same quality of the passively being involved. Regardless the fact that one should kill and the other should be killed, both the killer and victim appeared as passive agencies that followed the rules even against their desires. This explains the situation why a killer would kill even if he knew that he will be killed right after. I think that the semantic and mode of the expression "to fall in blood" used by both (the killer and victim) is a key of understanding the social context of the *gjakmarrja* situation; the same expression used by both the sides would question the highlanders' strong belief that killing was related to honor. The hero feeling is found nowhere, nor the aggressive feeling. From this expression, only the duty-feelings seems clear: "It is a duty ".

## TË BIESH NË GJAK- TO FALL IN BLOOD

The *gjakmarrja* stories among the Albanian highlanders are many and one might get wrong by the idea that killing and honor lived in symbiosis. First of all, not all the problems, feuds, and quarrels had the killing as the only contra part. The Kanun said, "Blood is blood and a fine is a fine" (p, 164) predicting a whole set of social sanctions and punishments other than the death penalty. All these cases were administrated by the council of the Elders, the representatives of which were the group of the chiefs of all the *shtëpia*-groups. It was the duty of the Elders to discuss the cases, to hear the persons involved including the witnesses, to admit the oath if it was the case, to give the punishment, and in general to make the arrangements of putting somebody's honor back. The pretence of the council was non revocable. Secondly, similar to other societies, there were crimes among the highlanders too. For them, the life and spirit of whom were almost "organically" tight to the weapons that they carried, it was easy that in blood boiling to push the riffle or gun out and to kill even not for any predicted reason. The boundaries were not always clear and this made sometimes the *gjakmarrja* cases endless particularly when they became as old as nobody could remember the first reason. More than human errors the endless bloodshed of *gjakmarrja* should be related not to the honor but control and politics over the insufficient arable land. This is one of the proofs that the scholars' studies of the end of the 19th Century and the beginning of the 20th Century describe and analyze the sunset of *gjakmarrja*. However, I believe there always was a clear distinction between a murder as a crime and a murder for the sake of honor to the collective conscience.

By the Kanun, the *killing* was considered as the right punishment that would wash the face and bring the honor back to the killer only in several known cases. It seems behind the doubt that every highlander that might hold a gun was able to kill or be killed but not all of them were for the sake of gjakmarrja. "The *Kanun* does not judge cases of violated hospitality, weapons, and adultery" (The Code of LD. p, 178). And only in these cases, by the *Kanun*, no one, including the Council of the Elders, had the right to judge the dishonored person in his decisions including that of the death penalty, too. However, any murder was a case of *gjakmarrja*: an eligible reason to start it, a dependable reason to continue, and a sufficient reason for reconciliation.

The fall in blood situation was a complex of very strict elements well defined by the *Kanun* ("The Kanun says...”). Thus, to determinate it, first of all, an eligible reason to start the *gjakmarrja* was required. Secondly, the *gjakmarrja* was always publicly announced. Thirdly, regardless the starting point that would include only two individuals, *gjakmarrja* was never individually restricted. The situation included at least two of the groups. It means that all the males, from both the families, could hold the free license to kill and to be killed by order, which, if it was not differently predicted (as it was in the case of violating the body of the victim, where him, who violated the body of the victim fell in blood twice) was strictly one by one from each side. The order was also publicly known, unforgettable and never mistaken even for generations.

The Kanun, to the Book Ten, The Law Regarding Crimes (pp: 154-186) not only gives in details the rights and obligations of both the sides during a possible conflict, but also preciously shows the movement path of the *gjakmarrja* as an solution of the dynamics of the rights and obligations . The article 914 said, “If someone threatens you or beats you and you kill him, you incur the [gjakmarrja]” (p, 174). Thus, the threat and the beat even considered as non honorable acts still were not sufficient reasons to apply the death penalty. These acts caused dishonor, but if the dishonored man killed the other one, the death, as a wrong solution of the case, was an eligible reason to start the *gjakmarrja*. Thus, he, instead of saving face incurred *gjakmarrja*. The article 828 said, “The gun brings blood to your house... The gun brings you into blood” (p, 162). In this case, the bearer of the weapon was obligated to repay with blood if he permitted his weapons to be used on taking blood. If the weapon used on the murder was taken without the bearer’s consent, then the murderer was obligated to repay with blood. There are also few other articles that totally clarified the situation. By the *Kanun* is said:

Blood follow the finger (p,172)

Blood is paid for with blood (p, 172)

A crime may not be recompensed with blood (p, 174)

Blood is not paid for with a fine (p, 174)

The gun pursues the murderer (p, 178)

He who kills himself is not avenged (p, 180).

According them it is clear that not any killing was for the sake of the honor nor such cases honored the killer. In contrast, every murder for the sake of the gjakmarrja was a drama of the individuals.

## APRIL-LOVE, APRIL-DEATH *...

To theoretically describe *gjakmarrja* as a social phenomenon it would always be hard, even impossible: Every *gjakmarrja* had its own case. Even though everything was strictly defied by the *Kanun*, the social environment (including the time and the place), the human sentiments, and especially the politics of the group and its position on the community made the *gjakmarrja* cases very variable. In this essay, I will analyze the elements of the *gjakmarrja* by the model given to the novel Broken April of the Albanian well known writer Ismail Kadare:

*"Gjorg' father, who had it from his own father, had told him the story of their enmity with the Kryeqyqe family. It was a story marked by twenty-two graves on each side, forty-four in all...*

*And all this had begun seventy years ago, on a cold had- night, when a man had knocked at their door, "Who was that man?" Gjorg had asked as a little boy, when for the first time he had heard the story of the knocking at the door. The question would be repeated many times time and* later on, and no one would ever answer it. For no one had ever known, who that man was. And even now, Gjorg could no believe that anyone has actually knocked at their door.

It was easier for him to imagine that a ghost had knocked, or fate itself, rather than an unknown traveler. The man, after knocking, had called from the gate and asked for shelter for the night. The head of the house, Gjorg's grandfather, had opened the door to him. They had welcomed him as was the custom, had brought him food and prepared him a bed, and early next morning, still according to custom, one of the family, his grandfather's younger brother, had escorted the unknown guest to the outer limits of the village. He had just left the man when he heard a shot. The stranger had fallen, dead, exactly at the border of the village lands.

Now, according to the Kanun, when the guest whom you were accompanying is killed before your eyes, you are bound to avenge him. But if he had been struck down after you had turned your back, you were free of that obligation. The man who had been escorting his guest had in fact turned his back before the man had been hit; therefore it was not his responsibility to avenge him. But no one had seen it happen. It was very early in the morning and no one in the neighborhood could testify in the matter. Even so, his protector's word would have been believed, since the Kanun trusts a man's word, and it would have been regarded as established that the man who had accompanied his guest had taken leave of him and turned his back by the time the killing had occurred, if another obstacle had not arisen. That was the orientation of the victim's body. The committee that was formed at once to determine if the duty of avenging the unknown guest fell to the house of Berisha, considered everything minutely, and concluded at last that the Berisha were indeed the ones who must avenge him. The stranger had fallen face down with his head towards the village. For that reason, according to the Code, the Berisha, who had, given the stranger shelter and had fed him, had had the duty to protect him until he left the village lands, and must now avenge him"

(*) Taken from the Broken April of Ismail Kadare. (1990. pp: 30-32)

This was the story that made the 22-year-old Gjorg a killer for the sake of the *gjakmarrja* for his killed brother. The novel describes his last thirty days- the days gifted by the thirty-day-*besa* given from the victim's group to him. He killed his brother's killer on the seventieth of the March. Gjorg would be finally killed by a member from the other group on the seventieth April. The April was broken in two halves as well as his fresh started life. April love, April-death; the same as the Albanian highlander's life that was always between life and death, death and reconciliation. He died leaving no body in his village surprised or angered. "They eyes showed no hatred. They were cold as the March day, as he himself had been cold, without hatred..." (Kadare,I. 1990: p, 15 ).

The analysis of Gjorg's gjakmarrja leads to three different steps, usually present to all these dramas. Step one: The conflict suddenly started where a member of the group (who, in this case, happen to be the guest) was killed. Step two: A conflict usually develops inside of the victim's group. As Hamlet said, the problem remained, "To be or not to be" (to give the *besa* or to ask for a blood payment). In this case, since the guest was killed when he was still in his host's borders and *besa*, it was the responsibility of the host's group to take the blood of the guest. Since the violation of the hospitality would be never a case of forgiveness, the host had no other choice but to ask for *gjakmarrje*. As we already said, a male member -which used to be a brother but in this case was one of the male members of the group found responsible to take blood- was picked based on the common consent. He knows that after the killing, it should be his turn. There is spiritual conflict inside him(Kadare, I. 1990: p, 19). Between life and death

(Aprillove, Aprildeath...) he wants to get the value of this killing. He seeks to get a good reason to kill. But everybody from the *shtëpia*-group is waiting for his final act. The blood stains in his brother's shirt began to yellow and everybody "knows" that this is a real sign that "the dead man was in tourment yearning for vendetta" (Kadare, I. 1990: p, 22). The community, however, seems to hold no knowledge about the spiritual conflict inside of Gjorg. Step three: The solution, as it may be thought, comes as another murder. Then, the community, even that had no knowledge for the inside conflict of individual, totally admits the new murder saving the young man from any further spiritual doubt. Furthermore the young man feels released from the voice of his dead brother that asked for the *gjakmarrja*. The blood-soaked shirt that the brother had worn at the day that he was killed, after a long time hanged, as the Kanun required, from the upper storey of the house, was finally washed as proving that what people said about blood stains. (Kadare,I. 1990: p, 22).

## RECONCILIATION

The conflict between the individual and the social side inside the pointed killer makes us thinking, that a second choice, at least theoretically, may always occur: Not to kill. Thus, it might be presume that the best choice would be the stop of the killing. I think it is obvious from what we have explained that there was no other choice in such cases, but only *gjakmarrja*. Another decision would mean to admit the group dishonor in eternity, which should be terrible for a highlander that lived only *për dy gisht nder* (for two fingers honor). The decision to stop killing without taking any other eligible action would be punished, as we said, by several social sanctions. However, between the families involved in the *gjakmarrja*, the reconciliation was a known practice and was defined also by the *Kanun*.

By the Kanun, the rule of *gjakmarrja* was strictly *one by one*. Based on the reciprocity principle, at this point the *gjakmarrja* situation would be considered mature and closed. Unfortunately, this was not always true. The *gjakmarrja* situation between two different groups, as we already explained, might last as long as different generations past through until no one could remember the first reason of starting and who's turn was. Thus, the "blood factory" produced gallons of blood. Only the turn was always strictly remembered. At this point, even though the *gjakmarrja* played a possible regulator of social cohesion, it might be said it was not rare for highlanders' community to totally lose its control over *gjakmarrja*. The Broken April with the forty-four *gjakmarrja* graves shows that other social forces were interested to illegally keep the blood machine running even though apparently this was based on the Code. However, after any killing, not only a state of reconciliation was always possible, but also was a requirement.

According the *Kanun* asking the victim's group for reconciliation was part of the ritual and custom of the *gjakmarrja*. Thus, right after killing, a mediator was sent from the gjaksi's group to his victim's group asking for the 24-hour-truce (*besa njëzetekatërorëshe*). By the Kanun, after the last murder, it was eligible to kill someone from the killer's group right way. The act was considered as a right solution in the blood-boiling situation (gjaknxehtësi- very hot blood). As Hasluck has been noticed, most of the killings for the sake of gjakmarrja were made during the blood boiling situation. "The truce is a period of freedom and security which the family of the victim gives to the murderer and his family, temporarily suspending pursuit of vengeance in the blood-feud until the end of the specified term" (The Code of LD. p, 165). The truce could be available for twenty-four hours or/and thirty days. If the group of the victim would give the twenty-four-hour truce, then the killer was free to attend the social occasion of mourning and burial of the victim. Not only the *Kanun* treated dishonoring, ignoring, and showing arrogance or hater during the mourning ceremony, from both sides, as ethical issues, but also prohibited them as against rules.

If the twenty-four-hour-truce was given, then another meeting was set between mediator and the victim's family in order to get a longer truce- *besa tridhjetëditëshe* (the thirty-day-truce). The *Kanun* says, "*Me çue gjind për besë asht kanu; me dhanë besë asht detyrë e burrni*- to ask somebody to mediate the truce is a requirement; to give the truce is obligation and honor" (The Code of LD. p, 165). The twenty-four-hour and thirty-day truces were agreements for a twenty-four-hour or thirty- day peace. In my knowledge, no murders were recorded during the *besa*-period that was intensively spent by the males of the killer's group to discharge their long term ordinary obligations. However, in this case the *Kanun* predicted a terrible set of sanctions for the violator and his group including the dismissal of the entire group.

If during that time, both sides, mediated by the mediator of blood concluded to a reconciliation agreement, the highlanders followed another set of rituals as the public declaration of the amnesty, the visits in groups starting from the last victim's house, eating the meal of the blood (eating meal in the victim's house), walking in all the rooms of the house upon the belief that "the last shadow of the feud must be driven out of every corner of the house" (Kadare, I. 1990: p, 48) and until to the ritual of drinking blood and giving *besa* to each-other. Since then, from the worse enemies the members of those groups would be called as brother and sisters. Their alliance would be never doubt. The marriages among them will be prohibited as the marriages inside the same group. Unfortunately, Gjorg had not a similar end. However, after the reconciliation the social cohesion developed to its next level.

# V

## THE ANTHROPOLOGY OF GJAKMARRJA (CONCLUSIONS)

Instead of being static, the social cohesion appears as the dynamics of affiliations, rights, and obligations always in change. The life of community as the record of the births, marriages, deaths, alliances, and wars accompanied in every stage by changeable obligations is always mobile and at the same time cohesive. Otherwise, the surviving would be destructed. In this terms, the social cohesion moves from a stage to another by the natural or forced changes among the social affiliations transferring without any lost the whole set of the obligations in different directions. To explain the place and role of *gjakmarrja* in this situation we need to employ different anthropological concepts. We also need to further elaborate the concepts of the individual, the group, and their relationship as a set of the mutual rights and obligations in order to keep the social cohesion.

Only by mistake we say community and think a group of people. If we start to analyze deeper the mutual relationship between individual and community as a group of people, the mistake is clear: We say "Me" and "They" thinking for them as the group of other people excluding "I". This is true for any of the individuals inside community. This proves that saying community, more than to a group of people we usually refer an imaginary group of people that only symbolically exists as such in our conscience. There is no doubt that group exists: people that by naturally or voluntarily affiliations share the same territory and agree for the same rules upon surviving. It seems, in the case of the Albanian highlanders there was a society that more than to the individual was based on the work and power of the entire group. Furthermore, the community by itself worked as an extended family of the different levels. I believe that this structure supports any idea of replacing the group as a physical entity with the group as identity; its culture, as a surviving technique. In our conscience, when we presume about what other people might say or think we do not refer to any of them in particular or to all of them as the total. Mostly we refer to "them" reminding similar practices of the group. The others (they-the community) come to our conscience only as an image. In few words, what we think as group or community is a past or learned experience: it is culture. I insist on "culture" because the term "group of people" is insufficient to understand the relationship between individual as a member of community and the community as a group of members that even is quite possible not to know each other at all interfere and even control the life of all the members.

The image of the "others" is early created to any human being who as such is always participating at least in its biological group. One might be voluntarily or involuntarily such a member: voluntarily when the individual decides and have the new group approval to be attached and involuntarily when the individual is born as a member of the group, or had moved in as a child as part of his biological group. Involuntarily attached I would also call the females that became members of another group because of their marriages. Being naturally born as such, or the mutual desire and consensus for a new attachment seem as requirements of being a new member of the group. However, voluntarily or involuntarily, to be a member of the group one should admit and follow the group rules. It seems any member hold a tacit agreement, written and said nowhere, but known well from the all: the agreement to respect the group existing culture. *Hidhi kёmbёt sipas muzikёs* (Dance by the music), is still said meaning that to be successful one might know and follow the rules.

In this context, I think that honor and being honored perfectly fit on the system. As we already said the honor was the social credit that the group gave to its members that promised to/and fulfilled their social obligations. We also said that the group was the entity of people "sworn" to discharge their social obligations. They also have agreed to all the sanctions (including the death penalty) in case of the violation. This is the soil of the Kanun: the soil of equality, reciprocity, solidarity and self-governance. All the members were evaluated equal upon their honorable status (a dishonored member was socially dead, *de jure* not a member). As Durkheim has noticed, reciprocity and solidarity are the main characteristics of the communities at this stage of the society. In order to survive, since the power of the individual was not sufficient, the life was always and totally based on the power of the group. The same reasons might have built this society as a perpetual self-controlled mobile with no need for hierarchy and bureaucracy. The self-governance was the mode of the working of this community: the way the community kept the social cohesion.

There were sanctions against the members that conflicted and violated the rules, obligations, and agreements. They were always based on the *Kanun*. There are recorded cases when the community decided to dismiss a wrongdoer and whole its family. The dismissed members never complained. It seems that they considered the dismissing as the right of the community or as a fatality. However, they had only a choice: To leave. This also proves the existence of the tacit agreement between the member and the group as an entity. The same as the Roman Law, the *Kanun* applied the sanction for the cases with a strong ethical background. There were also social sanctions tacitly announced. These were the worst sanctions ever: The social sanction that tacitly announces a member socially dead. Even though the "others" never talked, held any meeting, nor voted for such cases, they tacitly agreed to tacitly announce a member as socially dead.

Another proof of the social agreement between community and its members are the gossip and social opinion. If the group response does not come in time or does not follow the rules, it seems the community uses different tools to help the development of the situation. I would evaluate gossip and opinion as two social forces that attempt to control forces in the name of community. The opinion and gossip are two social forces that are automatically employed by community only in cases when there is a danger to lose its integrity, culture, and identity. Thus, the gossip is something that we can hear: People talking. The social opinion is something that we mostly feel from this talking or what we remember in analogy. In these societies, sharing the same territory was a great possibility to share the same survival techniques; the same ideas; and the same customs. Thus, the social opinion was a norm of living for the highlanders.

In this context, the *gjakmarrja* worked as a social obligation. Even though the conflict inside *Gjorg* seems that started spiritually and was individually raised, it appeared as a conflict between social and individual side inside of him. Following this terminology, the social side would be what any individual of [this pre-agricultural] community would feel or/and do at the same case. The individual side is how the situation would be individually evaluated and varied. In this case, it seems the social side was a partner on starting the conflict inside the individual. Even more, it was the social side that encourages, configures, and forces the spiritual conflict to produce another murder, starting right after the first murder and long before the second one would happen as a response. The winner of this conflict remains preciously the social side (inside individual) that brings another murder as a solution. Only the last part of this invisible story remains visible: The society admits the murder. Gjorg succeeded the taking of the blood fulfilling his duty. No one put shame on him as a killer. Instead, he became a man (*burrë*).

The main difference stands to the contrast between the first murder that had shocked community and the second one that was socially admitted. Thus, while the first murder was socially considered as a crime, it seems the second one comes as justice; as punishment that brings back the social cohesion and peace. I believe that in case of *gjakmarrja* , not only the second murder was admitted, but also it seems the whole community was anxiously waiting to happen: The second murder, based on the reciprocity principle, was considered obligated. As such, it was encouraged, configured, and forced by community itself. The *gjakësi* was usually "hired" by community to kill. The killer was only a "worker" of the "blood factory"; in exchange for the social service to his group he would earn a social credit. The payments were differently designed. Their equivalence was usually a social individual credit transferred to him through his group (being honored) or directly to him from the entire community (he became a hero). The payment was equal to saving face (faqja e bardhe) or regaining honor (Qofsh me nder). Also, it was considered as a spiritual relax of both the first victim and the second murderer spirits.

I hope it is clear by now why the community admits the second murder. Thus, if we would start from the beginning: The conflict germinated in the soil of wrongdoing (a member of the group killed). The conflict grew at the most tangible and weakest point of community. The conflict flourished as a sentiment (The change of the color of the blood stains on the clothes of the victim were thought as the barometer of his pain and cry for *gjakmarrje*) and finally, through all these sentiments a second murder came as a solution- The inside voice asking for *gjakmarrje* involves the conscience of individual to act and realize a new murder. (Initially I thought that some sentiments as love inside family, frustration from a loved one's death, the hate to enemies of the other side, the mystical anxiety were the sentiments that make the conflict to erupt to the most tangible and the weakest point, that I thought as an individual, mostly a brother or the father. In fact, it is the case of sentiments, but there are different kinds of sentiments: The fear of the community about any possible change in its surviving technique and the fear of the victim's group to lose face. Thus, the "most tangible and weakest point" was always the entire group- the killer was picked based on the social consent and maybe was the probable victim of the group of the last victim).

Following the same line it would be said that firstly, the murder of the guest caused the lost of social balance bringing social inequality and the sentiment of social justice. The community shows its solidarity employing the gossip and opinion asking for justice. Secondly, the other murder, usually pre-known and socially admitted, brought the social balance and equality back. This is the situation when a murder (the second one) was not considered (by community) as a murder but as the right and justice.

How might somebody make the distinction between "good and right" and "bad and wrong"? What
have brought the highlanders to the conclusion that
some of the deaths were "inevitable" and even more
desirable? What makes us thinking or asking a punishment even the death penalty? To come to the concept
of the *gjakmarrja* one must examines and valuates the
killing of a group member as a wrongdoing situation,
an inequality, and injustice. It is understandable no one
would catch these concepts outside of community and
its culture. The killing of a group member would be
understood as a wrongdoing based on the culture of
a community, the individuals of which hold the full
knowledge that them all, as the members of the same
group, share the same right of living. Only in this community, where the individuals equally share the right
of living, the killing of an innocent member would
be considered as inequality. Only in this community,
where people evaluate living as an equal human right
inside community, the killing of an innocent member
would be considered as injustice. And only in this cultural situation one might feel that he naturally bears
the right of *gjakmarrja* against one, who took advantage
to the right of the living against an equal member; and
only in this situation one would feel that not only the
taking blood is right, but also is an obligation.

Who bears the obligation? I would support the idea
of a double obligation between individual and community. What I strongly believe is that once there was an
obligation between victim and its community. In these
terms, the *gjakmarrja* belongs to community: It was the
group obligation to take the blood. The dishonor of the
innocent victim belongs to his entire group. In this case,
the murderer was just an employee from the inside and
for the dishonored group; the sentiments are naturally
employed by community to discharge this big obligation in its favor. In this situation, any other member in-

side of the obligated group is equally obligated. This is why the gjakësi was always picked based on the common consent or even voluntarily. The social admission of the second murder, caused by the principle of the self- governance, proves that this time, the murderer was not the individual but the entire group.

# VI

## EPILOGUE

Even though the **gjakmarrja** remained history for more than forty years of the communist regime, the *gjakmarrja* stories among highlanders in few past years became the Albanian media scoops. There are daily murders recorded as *gjakmarrja* cases. Only a few weeks ago one of the local representatives of the Shkodra city, after two years being a "prisoner" of the *gjakmarrja* inside his home, finally left the country. Recently there was ordinary news in one Albanian newspaper ( Gazeta Shqiptare, Mars 15, 2003). It was said,

*"How an ex-policeman became a killer... The gjakmarrja pushed an ex-policeman of the Puke police station became a killer. The 44-year old Frrok Lleshi is listed as a criminal after a murder in*

*the year of 1995, where he took blood for his brother that was killed by rivals. The gjakmarrja virus is really crazy. Preciously this virus has recruited on the crimes list the ex-policeman... changing the path of his life *".*

After the deaths of his killed brother and son in different times, *Frrok Lleshi* has killed two other people.

Recently he became suspicious for another murder: The family of the victim *Tom Gjergji* accuses their cousin, *Frrok Lleshi* as the author of the crime. The article author said, "All these crimes stories complicate the position of the ex-employee of the *Pukë* police-station. Regarding justice authorities, *Lleshi* risks to spend the rest of his life in prison".

It is quite understandable that regardless the fact those killers might be criminals or ex-policemen, all the murders are already crimes. The Durkheim said, "... We must not say that an action shocks the conscience collective because it is criminal, but rather that it is criminal because it shocks the conscience collective. We do not condemn it because it is a crime, but it is a crime because we condemn it" (1972, p.123-124). We already proved that this was quite true even in the traditional society of the Albanian highlanders where the *gjakmarrja* was realized as social obligation.

If in this essay to explain the gjakmarrja as social obligation among the Albanian highlanders we used as a strong reference the social-cultural environment of the traditional life, using similarly the same reference, it should be admitted that the structure that held the strong web-obligation is totally changed. The Albanian society is successfully integrating to the international free market system. Albania has a democratic parliament, modern governing, and constitution by contemporaneous parameters. The Albanians have a new life style. Even in the very isolated area of the highland, people have constructed their own houses drastically reducing the number of the households on the members of the biological family: Parents and children. The arranged marriages are no longer preferred, even though are still acceptable.

On the other side, a considerable number of the Albanian girls it is said that work as prostitutes in other

European countries. The crime inside the family is in the highest level ever. All these facts clearly show that the group has lost its power over its members. The relationship between the individual and the *shtëpia*-group is exhausted. The traditional social structure is totally changed and the social sanctions are no longer into play. The perpetual system based on equality, solidarity, reciprocity and self-governance is corrupted. The Albanian citizens are equal in front of the law, but they are no longer equal regarding their social status, education, and wealth. Thus, the gjakmarrja has lost its socio-cultural environment. The Albanian highlanders' community has no longer need for the *gjakmarrja*. There are no longer supportive proofs for the gjakmarrja. If any scholar demands that *gjakmarrja* is in the Albanian genes, beyond any scientific falsification also shows a total ignorance in the Albanian history and culture.

There is no renaissance, but reminiscence of the *gjakmarrja*. Being very long part of the Albanian life, the *gjakmarrja* was culturally designed. There are still people that believe to *gjakmarrja* even though do not understand it. There are other people who with or without knowledge confuse the sentiment for vendetta with vendetta as social obligation. This became truer in the case of *gjakmarrja*: It is obvious that crime is appeared wearing the archaic *gjakmarrja* clothes hoping to survive in its cultural roots. However, regardless media speculations, I think that Albanian juridical system plays no longer the precedent of the *gjakmarrja*.

# VII

## APPENDIX

*Beja*-The oath

*Besa*-The word of pledge

*Buka e gjakut* (*The bread of blood*) -The blood meal.

*Faqja e bardhe*(The white cheek)-Used in terms of saving face. *Faqebardhë* was used for an honored person

*Faqja e zeze* (The black cheek)- Used in terms of losing face. *Faqezi* was the synonym of the dishonored person

*Fisi*-Clan

*Gjakmarrja* ( *blood taking*) -A form of blood feud

*Gjaksi* ( From the Albanian gjak [blood], since the gjaks is fulfilling his duty under the provisions of the Kanun ) -The killer in a gjakmarrja's situation

*I zoti i gjakut*-The master of blood

*Kulla e gjakut*-A tower without windows where a man who has killed may seek permanent refuge, and be maintained indefinitely with food and drink set just inside door.

*Kulla*-A stone dwelling in the form of a tower, peculiar to the mountain regions of Albania

*Kumbara-* The godfather of hair or the baptism

*Larja e gjakut-*The wash of blood.

*Mikpritja-*The hospitality

*Miku-*The guest

*Nderi-* honor

*Pleqesia-* The Elders

*Rrofsh!* (May you be alive) An Albanian wish in terms of thanking someone or in other enthusiastic situation

*Taksa e gjakut-* The tax of blood

*Te biesh ne gjak* -To fall in blood

*Trim-* The hero

*Tungjatjeta!*("Long life to you")-An Albanian greeting used when people meet each other in occasional situations

*Vellazeria-* The brotherhood

*Vllami-* Brother by choice. A person from another clan declared as a brother in a given circumstances and considered as a biological siblings.

# VIII

## BIBLIOGRAPHY

Broughton, J.C. 1971. A Journey through Albania and Other Provinces of Turkey in

Europe and Asia, to Constantinople During the Years 1809 and 1810. Eastern

Europe Collection". Arnos Press& The New York Times, NY. USA.

Boehm, C. 1984. Blood Revenge The Anthropology of Feuding Montenegro And

Other Tribal Societies. The University Press of Kansas, Lawrence Kansas.USA.

Hasluck, M. 1954. The Unwritten Law In Albania. Edited by J. H. Hutton. Cambridge

At the University Press, USA.

Mauss, M. 1990. The Gift. The Form and Reason For Exchange in Archaic Societies.

Translated by W.D.Halls. Foreword by M. Douglas. Published by Routledge In Great Britain.

Durham, E. 2000. High Albania A Victorian Traveler's Balkan Odyssey. With Intr.

by John Hodgson. Published by Phoenix Press, USA.

Trix, F. 2001. Albanians in Michigan. "Discovering people of Michigan" Michigan

State University Press, East Lansing, USA.

Weber, M. 2001. The Protestant Ethic and Spirit of Capitalism. First published by Routledge 1992. London. NY, USA.

McGee, R. J. and Warms, L R. 2000. Anthropological Theory An Introductory

History. First Edition 1996, Mayfield Publishing Company. Mountain View, CA, USA.

Sonnichsen, L. C. 1957. Ten Texas Feuds. University of New Mexico. Press

Albuquerque. New Mexico. USA.

_____1962. I'll Die Before I'll Run. The Story Of The Great Feuds Of

Texas. The Devin-Adair Company. NY, USA.

Jones, V. C. 1948. The Hatfields And The McCoys. The University of North Carolina Press. North Carolina, USA.

Kadare, I. 1990. Broken April. Translated from the Albanian New Amsterdam

Books.Lanham, MD, USA.

_____ 1981. Vepra Letrare. V12. [Red. D. Dilaveri], Sh B "Naim Frasheri", Tirana, Albania.

Armstrong, H. 2001. Gjashtë Muaj Mbretëri 1914 Kujtime, Sh B "Onufri". Tirana, Albania.

Shuflaj, M. 2002. Serbët Dhe Shqiptarët Historia E Shqiptarëve Të Veriut. Sh B "Bargjini". Tirana, Albania.

The Code of Lekë Dukagjini. 1989. Albanian text with parallel English Translation by Leonard Fox. Gjonlekaj Publishing Co. NY. USA.

The Dictionary of Anthropology. 2002. Edited by Thomas Barfield

Blackwell Publishers Ltd First published 1997. USA

Before the Rain (film), directed by Milcho Manchevski

http://durkheim.itgo.com/crime.html

http://durkheim.itgo.com/solidarity.html

http://durkheim.itgo.com/assorteddurkheim.html

http://www.src.uchicago.edu/ssr1/PRELIMS/Theory/weber.html

http://www.boston.com/dailyglobe2/343/focus/In_Kosovo_dying_
    by_the_Code_= +.shtml

http://www.balkanweb.com/gazeta/faqe 16-17/4.htm

http://www.freep.com/news/locoak/nalban1_20030401.htm

# Gjakmarrja, Albanian Highlander's "Blood Feud" as Social Obligation

*A review of Diana Gellçi's book*
by **Bjoern Andersen**

Recently, Diana Gellçi - an Albanian anthropologist with relations to the Albanian Institute for International Studies in Tirana - published an essay on the Albanian "Blood Feud". The focus is on the content and impact of the old customary law – known as the kanún - in Northern Albania and Kosova. To foreign readers with some knowledge of Albanian history and social life in the Northern highlands it is a good companion - maybe an eye-opener too.

We do not know much about the origin of the kanún, but there might be an ancient nucleus, since there are many similarities to customary law in other parts of the world, in Italy and Corsica for instance - and also in old Nordic societies, in Norway, Iceland and Denmark.

In the 15th century the old customary Albanian laws were somehow collected; the most famous collection was made on the order of Lekë Dukagjin, one of the medieval Albanian princes;

another collection was made in the district of Scanderbeg, maybe not exactly on his order.

Possibly Dukagjin invited elders and leading villagers to gatherings to reach some sort of a consensus.

In all the years of the Ottoman Empire the Albanian highlanders upheld the kanún as a living oral tradition and some foreigners who paid visits to Albania – among those Edward Lear in the

mid 19th century and Edith Durham in the first part of the 20th century – have made informative notes about it. In the first part of the 20th century, the catholic Albanian priest, Shtjefën Gjeçov, collected the kanún as it had survived in the Northern highlands. It is his collection and arrangement scholars and writers mostly refer to when they nowadays write about old customary law, and Diana Gellçi is no exception.

## ORAL TRADITION AND WRITTEN EDITION

We have to bear in mind a major difference between an oral tradition and a written edition, and that is the arrangement. Possibly, we may have to take the oral tradition as detached stories or specific cases built upon some ancient principles of reciprocity. If there is a structure or a hierarchy in the oral tradition it is not that firm or in that way as in a written arrangement. When the elders in the villages were discussing and deciding in a conflict, they may have made their references like this: The kanún says ..., that is: When we are applying our recollection of similar cases on the specific circumstances, we have to decide in this way now. They did not refer to a well-edited law, nor to specific articles, they referred, I imagine, to cases and stories, similar to the tradition of Homeric story-tellers in Greece.

## CATHOLIC INFLUENCE

For long periods the customary laws most likely were unchanged in general. But something very important have happened in medieval times and that was the emerging influence of the catholic church - both on the Princes and on the ordinary people in the highlands. Maybe this influence already had reached a culmination at the time of Dukagjin and Scanderbeg, maybe that

happened later on. In the Gjeçov-collection from the first part of the 20th century the old tradition and the catholic influence have been mingled - and a very special balance has been established. Since medieval times the catholic church has been against feuds and taking blood, in the Gjeçov-collection feuds and taking blood still is a living tradition in general, but if a catholic priest was killed, the punishment was that harder.

## BALANCE ACCOUNTS. MEDIATION

Taking blood was not the only response to a severe offence, but quite a "natural" one – an eye-for-an-eye response as in the Old Testament. Definitely, taking blood was meant to "balance accounts" when some family or clan had been offended, but also – I imagine – to prevent other offences in the future.

Furthermore, the kanún says quite a lot about mediation and reconciliation. Whether this has to be seen as an ancient tradition or it is a consequence of catholic influence I do not know, but possibly it is a tradition of some age. To what degree the village elders succeeded in mediating in conflicts or even hindering their escalation we do not know, but many conflicts did not stop - and countless males were killed.

## DIANA GELLÇI'S SOURCES

Diana Gellçi has not made studies of her own, her sources are the Gjeçov-collection, the writings of Edith Durham and Margaret Hasluck and the famous novel of Ismail Kadaré –

"Broken April". All these books are highly relevant, but they have to be interpreted differently, and I do not think that the author has discussed that thoroughly enough. The first three books are the results of a systematic collection of observations and of evidence from informants - and it would have been nice, if the author had made some considerations about the collection process and of the arrangement-process too.

## THE KADARÉ NOVEL

Ismail Kadaré at the conference about 'Clash of Civilizations', Tirana 2003. Photo: Bjoern Andersen The novel is quite another thing, an artistic interpretation of tradition in which a certain

point-of-view, the point-of-view of an individual, is introduced - but actually in a very complex and maybe modern way. The novel can not be read in the same way as Gjeçov, Durham and

Hasluck, it can not be read straightforward so to speak. We have to take the individualistic point of view in the novel cum grano salis, with a grain of salt, since one of the main characteristics of the kanún is collectivity and collective responsibility, and not at all personal viewpoints or individualistic behaviour.

Individualistic behaviour seems in tradition to have been understood as an exception – which in some occasions even had to be punished. As I read Kadaré it is one of his major points that individualistic behaviour – under the given circumstances – was out of question, it did not - as in the time of Hoxha - have any relevance. In the novel the young man had to kill another one, and was to be killed himself, just to uphold social order.

## FAMILY

To my knowledge Diana Gellçi is quite right when she is taking the family as the most simple and constituent element in traditional highland life – definitely not a family of modern type or a democratic entity, but a kinship one. When she is speaking about reciprocity, she often also speaks about equality and solidarity; again I will suggest to take it cum grano salis – since this equality possibly not were between two "common" individuals, but between two families, two kins etc. - maybe sometimes between two persons at the top of the hierarchy, who were not taken as individuals but as representatives.

Diana Gellçi has characterized the role of the females as inferior to the role of the males, but most likely many of the males were in inferior positions too, especially if the household kept male servants. Furthermore, many of the male Albanians did not become master of a house, and therefore they often were subordinates to their grandfather, their father or an elder brother all through their life.

Kanún has not exactly been swept away because of social development; only at the time of the Hoxha-regime the authorities succeeded in suppressing customary law. It was written in the "Tirana Times" 4th June 2005 that as much as 734 families in Northern Albania actually are involved in blood feuds. Hopefully traditional blood feuds will disappear by mediation and reconciliation - or by "desvetudo", that is when a blood feud not any longer is a proper way to solve a severe conflict among ordinary people.

From time to time Albanian media tell about modern feuds – feuds in the dark, feuds between criminals. To Diana Gellçi these modern feuds have not very much in common with the traditional feuds. I agree in that, that is to some extent. On the other hand, if you are studying the dark areas of society – maybe in the context of acting against organized crime and trafficking - it will be helpful to know something about traditional life, not only in Albania but in other past societies too.

## Customary law and government

Customary law – or local, independent and traditional rule - has often persisted when the Government was weak, distant or ignorant, it has been said. For long periods that might have been the situation in the Albanian highlands and in Kosova, for example in periods when the Sultan did not want to or was not able to control the Albanians in detail but only in some areas, cities and mostly in plain field.

Anyway, the situation when no state and no government has been established - and the situation when a weak state or King is in "power" are quite different.

In medieval Denmark the King aimed at controlling the society and protecting it, that was his raison d'être. He could not do that alone, he had to come to agreement with the nobles, and in that course he and the nobles collected and re-constructed old customary law and published new common law. The articles about beehives, fish traps and water mills were only modified slightly since all agreed in them and in the necessity of such articles, the articles about revenge and ordeal by fire were radically modified because of clerical influence.

In the next hundreds of years economy and society developed, struggles for power went on from time to time – and first after some 4-500 years and a major defeat in the wars against the Swedish King, the Danish King was able to establish himself as an absolute monarch (in cooperation with some nobles and members of the upcoming classes of merchants etc.). Then in 1683 he issued a new common law of his own. Some elements of the customary law were integrated in this new law, some of them abolished – and there was not any longer doubt about the King's overall monopoly in criminal law. So, in Danish history customary law has either been integrated in the law process and been modified - or has been abolished. And some parts have "expired" by desvetudo.

After a great political crisis in the mid of the 19th century, the Danes began to establish a democratic society and new customary law - and that law is in many aspects distinct from the medieval law and the law of 1683.

Most Danes accept parliamentary law, they even want it enforced, the dark forces punished and taken into custody - and the dark spots "enlightened". But in some limited and sinister "parts" of Danish society, the areas of biker gangs and of drug traffickers, modern "clan law" actually is in force.

## THE ALBANIAN HISTORY

In Albania history has been quite different from Danish history. Possibly some elements of customary law have been integrated in – and modified by – modern law; many other elements may officially have been abandoned, but have persisted in some periods - and in the most "remote" parts of the country.

But since government in many aspects has been weak after the break-down of the Hoxha-regime - and since economic conditions are so poor, a new, big and dark society has been developed beside the "official" one. In this new parallel society – which is estimated to cover about 60% of the Albanian economy – a new customary law is being established. Some of the "articles" are, I imagine, rules of old age built upon the principle of reciprocity and upon an ancient code of honour. But more of the "articles" are new, built upon principles of hierarchy and power.

Here is much to study - and much to worry about.

*Bjoern Andersen*

This Kanun existed only in oral form and was first codified by Lekë Dukagjini in the 15th century. The code was written down only in the 19th century by Shtjefën Gjeçovi and partially published in the Hylli i Drites periodical in 1913. The full version appeared only in 1933 after Gjeçovi's death in 1926. In 1989 a dual English-Albanian version was published. and then replicated in a 1992 version.

Although Kanuni is attributed to the Albanian prince Lekë Dukagjini, the rules evolved over time as a way to bring laws and rule to these lands. The code was divided into the following 12 books (or sections): Church, Family, Marriage, House, Livestock and Property, Work, Transfer of Property, Spoken Word, Honor, Damages, Law Regarding Crimes, Judicial Law, Exemptions and Exceptions.

The Kanun has 1,262 articles which regulate all aspects of the mountainous life: economic organization of the household, hospitality, brotherhood, clan, boundaries, work, marriage, land, and so on. The Besa (honour) is of prime importance throughout the code as the cornerstone of personal and social conduct.

Some of the most controversial rules of the Kanun (in particular book 10 section 3) specify how murder is supposed to be handled. The Albanian name for blood feud is Gjakmarrja.

**The Kanun is based on four pillars:**

**Honour** *(Albanian:* **Nderi***)*
**Hospitality** *(Albanian:* **Mikpritja***)*
**Right Conduct** *(Albanian:* **Sjellja***)*
**Kin Loyalty** *(Albanian:* **Fis***)*

*The Kanun of Lekë Dukagjini is composed of 12 books and 1,262 articles. The books and their subdivisions are the following:*

1.   Church;
         a.   The Church
         b.   Cemeteries
         c.   Property of the Church
         d.   The Priest
         e.   Church workers

2.   Family;
         a.   The family make-up

3.   Marriage;
         a.   Engagement
         b.   Wedding
         c.   The Kanun of the groom
         d.   In-laws
         e.   Separation
         f.   Inheritance

4. *House, Livestock and Property;*
    a.    *The house and its surroundings*
    b.    *Livestock*
    c.    *Property*
    d.    *The boundary*

5. *Work;*
    a.    *Work*
    b.    *Hunting*
    c.    *Commerce*

6. *Transfer of Property;*
    a.    *Borrowing*
    b.    *Gifts*

7. *Spoken Word;*
        8.    *Honor;*
    a.    *Individual honor*
    b.    *Social honor*
    c.    *'Blood' and gender; brotherhood and godparents*

9. *Damages;*

10. *Law Regarding Crimes*
    a.    *Criminals*
    b.    *Stealing*
    c.    *Murder (discussion of sanctioning of blood feuds)*
11. *The kanun of the elderly*

12. *Exemptions and Exceptions*
    a.    *Types of exceptions*
    b.    *Death*

Lekë Dukagjini is a quite complex historical figure. Furthermore, this figure has also taken dimension of a myth, if the term is accepted when our National Hero Gjergj Kastrioti-Scanderbeg is regarded.

Lekë Dukagjini (1410-1481) was contemporary with Gjergj Kastrioti (1405-1468). History has known both of them as hereditary princes, who were heightened when they took reins of their respective homonymous princedoms: Leka - the Dukagjnini's, when his father, Pal Dukagjini died, (1446) and Gjergj - the Kastrioti's, eight years after his father's, Gjon Kastrioti, death (1443). Dukagjini's Princedom, with Lezha as its own capital city, included Zadrima, the areas in north and northeast of Shkodra and was extended in remote areas of present Serbia, having Ulpiana, near Prizren, as e second capital city. On the other hand, Kastrioti's Princedom, with Kruja as its capital, included Mat and Dibra region, reaching Rodon Castle on the Adriatic coast. Since before coronation Lekë Dukagjini had gained a comprehensive education under the spirit of Europian Renaissance in cities like Venice, Raguza or Shkodra; meanwhile Scanderbeg had achieved a fast and splendid military career in the Sultan's court of Istanbul. Leading the Lezha League (founded in Lezha in 1444) Scanderbeg sow Leka (initially his father Pal Dukagjini) beside him. They fought side by side (sometimes they opposed each other) until Scanderbeg died (1468). Lekë Dukagjini continued his deed leading Albanians in most difficult period of their anti-ottoman resistance, till the end of his life (1481).

Chroniclers and historians, beginning from contemporary Tivarasi/ Biemi, Frëngu, Barleti e Muzaka, up to Gegaj and

Noli of 20-th Century, when enlightening the deeds of Gjergj Kastrioti, have rightly mentioned Lekë Dukagjini and other princes of that time. But we cannot say that they are right when groundlessly defamed Lekë Dukagjini, only because were enchanted by the by the main figure, Scanderbeg. Those anonymous, authors of myths have been more balanced. They identified Scanderbeg with a dragon-prince that, dared to fight and always to win against the monster, while they depicted Lekë Dukagjini as angel-prince, who, with courage and wisdom safeguards the continuity of Albanian cause.

Lekë Dukagjini was the most powerful Albanian prince after Scanderbeg. That is why his name became objective of intrigues by Venetian policy (and history) until La Signoria felt the risk from High Gate coming to the doorstep and really joined its forces with the Albanian resistance, declaring war to Ottoman Empire (1463). After that the Venetians ceased defaming Lekë Dukagjini. Its historians wrote for some deeds of Lekë Dukagjini, beside Scanderbeg until his death (1468) and later leading the Albanian troops beside Venetian forces until the sign of peace by Signoria and High Gate (1479). Afterwards they kept silence. Legend informs us that Lekë Dukagjini continued the resistance leading brave people of Princedom until his death.

The historians have defamed the name of Leke Dukagjin since the beginning, looking at him an antagonist personality to Scanderbeg, in order to make their stories about Scanderbeg, who was the only Albanian Hero, who Europe knew in the successful battles of Albanians against Ottoman invasion, more intriguing; but also because these historians refuse to blame Western Europe for not organizing an antiottoman coalition in the Balkans. They didn't dare to judge especially the Republic of Venice, which not only didn't stand allied to the Albanians when they were confronting an whole empire which was threating Europe, but made use of Albanian resistance for its commercial interests, intriguing to divide Albanian princes, making them confront each other with arms, or, when this was not possible, declaring them enemies of Venice and even of Christianity. Lekë Dukagjini *was the most powerful and authoritative prince, second only to Scanderbeg; that is why he became objective of intrigues by the Venitian policy (and historians), until Signoria felt the Ottoman threat coming to its gate and joined forces with the Albanian resistance, declaring war to Instambul (1463). After that year the Venitian defamation towards Lekë Dukagjini was ceased. In the meantime historians described some deeds of Lekë Dukagjini beside Scanderbeg until Scanderbeg died (1468) and later leadindg Albanian troops in battles side by side with Venitian forces, until Venice made peace with High Gate (1479). Afterwards historians were silent. The legends inform us that Lekë Dukagjini continued his resistance until his death.*

*But defamation towards Lekë Dukagjini's name has continued even after his death, as the resistance in his Princedom and more extensively continued. The defamation after death has to do with his work Kanun, that Lekë Dukagjini left as inheritance to his subordinates, Albanians. The essence of Kanun of Lekë Dukagjini are his sentences kept and enriched generation after generation for nearly six centuries. This Homeric phenomenon has raised his name to a legend, turned it in a genuine myth, to a degrre that make difficult for scholars to accept it as e historical reality. That explains why some of them have continued to defame Lekë Dukagjini's name and his Kanun, as happened to Homer and his Iliad and Odyssey. (For similarity: even to Lekë Dukagjini was invented a blind brother). But the time and circumstances when the sentences of Kanun were conceived can be enlightened analysing documented biographical facts for Lekë Dukagjini.*

*By the end of 50-ies of 15-th century, Dukagjini Princedom had not any more any of its developed centres: Lezha was surrendered to Venetians (1393), Ulpiana, the capital of Princedom was destroyed to the soil by the Turks, since before Prizren, a developed centre of Princedom, was surrendered to them (1458). Under those circumstances Lekë Dukagjini seized the fortress of Shati in Zadrima, intending to have it as his princely residence, but he was attacked by*

Skanderbeg, who handed it back to Venetians. Without a princely residence and, for some time, being amidst three fires (Turks, Venetians, Skanderbeg) Lekë Dukagjini found shelter in the hinterland of Highlands of his Princedom, where he constructed fortresses and castles togother with the free inhabitants of those areas, who warmly welcomed and respected their overlord of Dukagjini Family, his lady, Teodora of Muzakaj from Berat and all his court. With highlanders of Princedom, well-known for their bravery, Leka, not only rebuilt his castle-towns, but to ensure to himself a permanent source for a sufficient army, which played an important role within framework of Lezha League Army under Skanderbeg in command and even later. In exchange Lekë Dukagjini guaranteed to the highlanders of the Princedom and to everyone who, especially after the death of Scanderbeg, joined him for procuring a defence to himself, freedom within their tribal organisation, which he, under the circumstances, raised to the institutional level by reorganizing the Councils of Elders on village and region basis. Kanuni got conceived during this period (1458-1481), when he leaded all the popular assemblies and Councils of Elders and was inherited generation after generation as a practice of judgement and, using sentences formulated by him or restated case by case, as juridical sentences. Kanun, remained unwritten, but was acting in centuries as English "Common Law" acted, until was gathered and codified by Shtjefën Gjeçovi during replacement of 19-th with the 20-th century.

When Gjeçovi was working on the gathered canon material, Kanuni, as its author were sanctified by all the Albanians, regardless their religion. The name of Lekë Dukagjini was not defame by the people; on the contrary, it was hightened to a hero's level. The fact that a ruler turned to become a real, popular and national hero, could be explained by the theory which sustains that common people, accepting their rulers or knights as their heroes, "identified themselves with values of the leader and of the nobility, or, at least, because they needed to structure their world through models *offered by the ruling group" (P. Burke: 169)*

*Kanuni of Lekë Dukagjini is an unique work in Albanian with the humanist spirit of European Renaissance period, which, despite the fact that was and still is defamed, remains valuated highly by serious scholars, both Albanian and foreign as an "monumental work" (A. Buda/ Gjeçovi-Kryeziu: 22), "contribution in the treasure of world culture" (C. Von Scherwin/Hylli i Dritës 1929: 502) and its author, Lekë Dukagjini is qualified a "imposing personality" (Edith Durham: 116 and "National Hero" of its people. (J. Hahn: 114) A lot of writers and artists dedicated their works to him; among them the novelist and poet Ditëro Agolli ("Wife, for you I fought with Lekë Dukagjini", poetry), the Arbëresh dramatist Anton Santori ("Alessio Ducagini", melodrama, written between 1855-1860, published in 1983), the painter Naxhi Bakalli ("Kuvendi i Dukagjinit", tablo on the wall 4x3,2m in Burrel Historicaly Museum), the painter of Kosovo Engjëll Berisha ("Rrënjët e Dukagjinit", vizatime 1950-1956), the painter Simon Rrota (Lekë Dukagjini, portrait-Art Gallery, Shkodër), the sculptor Sotir Kosta ("Lekë Dukagjini", portrait in bronze in National Museum of Scanderbeg, Kruja, 1982) ect.*

*As apocrypha of Lekë Dukagjini is accepted the portrait of Simon Rrota (1887-1961), which introduce the author of Kanun in frontal view, having a sharp look, in which are joined together intelligence and wisdom, wearing the traditional waistcoat of costume of Albanian highlanders and a sword, holding a manuscript of Kanun in his left hand, which reminds the humanist intellectual of 15-th century. "An extraordinary personality", Lorenzo de Medici, with whom we wanted to compare Lekë Dukagjini since the beginning of this biography, was mentioned as "a genial politician, who could see the difference between the genuine power and its appearance". In the cover of his book he is depicted in the streets of Florence dressed as an ordinary citizen, encircled by girls singing his ballads... Lorenzo was really a good poet and the most generous patron of poets, scientists, and philosophers" (K, Clark: 106). To some extent,* we can imagine like that even Lekë Dukagjini, whose poetry would be his sentences of Kanun. If this comparison, as every other comparison, would not be accepted, we, at least, can compare the Dukagjini Princedom with the small courts of Northern Italy in the last quarter of the 15-th century, to whom "the Renaissance owes nearly as much as Florence" (K. Clark: 107). In this case Leka could be compared with Duke of Urbino, Frederigo Montefeltro, who "was not only a man of extraordinarily learning and cleverness, but also the greatest strategist of his time, who managed to defend his possessions from surrounding criminals. He was a passionate collectioner of books and, in his valuable portraits, he is depicted reading one of his manuscripts. He is wearing armor and other military equipment... His palace was initially being built as an fortress on a insurmountable rock and only later, after having procured safety, was given this soft and refined look, which made of it one of most beautiful architectonic monuments in the world" (K.Clark: 107).

We are able nowadays to restore neither a castle nor a princely palace of Leka Dukagjini; far less we can evaluate what does not exist with superlatives:" the most beautiful in the world, in Mediterranean, or in the region", because by that time " Albania was cancelled from the list of independent countries... every link with Europe was interrupted. Castles and flourishing cities... with palaces and monuments... were disappeared from the earth... remained as shadows of the ancient splendour. (F.S.Noli: 591-592). But Kanuni of Lekë Dukagjini is really the most important monument of Albanian culture during period of European Renaissance, which has lived for 6 centuries, playing such a extraordinary role in the life of the nation, of whose language is written.

**Dr. Tonin Cobani**